SECOND ED

HOW TO BUY A HOUSE, CONDO, OR CO-OP

Michael C. Thomsett
and the Editors of
Consumer Reports Books

Consumer Reports Books
A Division of Consumers Union
Yonkers, New York

For Jean

The goal of this book is to provide the home-buying consumer with basic and general information concerning the purchase of a family home, condominium, or cooperative apartment. The advice contained herein is intended for educational purposes only. Because laws, customs, and practices may vary from state to state, readers are urged to seek appropriate professional advice with regard to any specific real estate transaction.

Copyright © 1996 by Michael C. Thomsett and Consumers Union of United States, Inc., Yonkers, New York 10703.

Published by Consumers Union of United States, Inc., Yonkers, New York 10703.

All rights reserved, including the right of reproduction in whole or in part in any form.

Thomsett, Michael C.
    How to buy a house, condo, or co-op/Michael C. Thomsett and the
editors of Consumer Reports Books. — 2nd ed.
       p.   cm.
    Includes index.
    ISBN 0-89043-833-1
    1. House buying. 2. Condominiums. 3. Apartment houses,
Cooperative.   I. Consumer Reports Books.   II. Title.
HD1375. T534   1996   95-26711
  643'.12—dc20   CIP

Design by Joseph DePinho

First printing, March 1996

This book is printed on recycled paper.

Manufactured in the United States of America

How to Buy a House, Condo, or Co-op, Second Edition is a Consumer Reports Book published by Consumers Union, the nonprofit organization that publishes *Consumer Reports*, the monthly magazine of test reports, product Ratings, and buying guidance. Established in 1936, Consumers Union is chartered under the Not-for-Profit Corporation Law of the State of New York.

The purposes of Consumers Union, as stated in its charter, are to provide consumers with information and counsel on consumer goods and services, to give information on all matters relating to the expenditure of the family income, and to initiate and to cooperate with individual and group efforts seeking to create and maintain decent living standards.

Contents

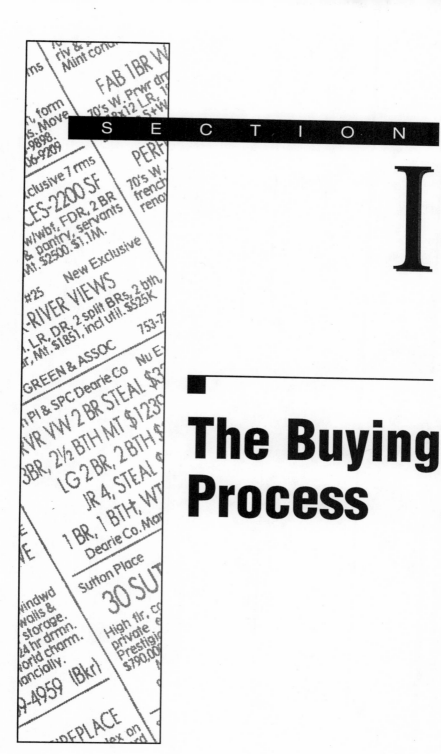

I

The Buying Process

1

Owning Your Own Home

Home ownership is the essence of the American Dream. We are raised to believe in the value of real estate and to recognize home ownership as a sign of success. It is also the most momentous financial decision we'll ever make.

From early childhood, we are told that owning a piece of land is a very American idea. We are plied with stories of plucky pioneers who carved homesteads out of the primeval forests and, later, out of the prairies and deserts of the Southwest. Even Thomas Jefferson asserted that a nation of small landowners was essential in a flourishing democracy.

Evidently, Jefferson's theory has caught on. According to the Bureau of the Census, about 60 million Americans own and live in their own homes, condos, or co-ops.

Without a doubt, owning your own home can provide great personal satisfaction, a feeling of pride, and a sense of success. Home ownership represents visible evidence of financial and personal accomplishment; it's a sign that you have "made it." The sense of security in owning your own shelter is nothing to be scoffed at either. In fact, most home buying is largely motivated by these kinds of intangible benefits. In addition, some of the tangible benefits of home ownership include tax deductions, increasing property values, and a fixed-housing cost. All of these are strong financial incentives for home ownership.

Whereas the rewards may eventually be substantial, the actual process of home buying can be long and arduous. Initially, the search for a suitable, affordable home can be exhausting and time-consuming, and negotiating the right price, mortgage terms, and other contractual conditions can be full of pitfalls for the novice home buyer. Real estate agents and attorneys can be a big help in this regard, especially with home inspection and the intricate closing procedures that require a good deal of knowledge. Owning a home is a long-term financial commitment (as long as 30 years), and maintenance and upkeep of a house and grounds is a constant expense in time and money, usually far above the expense renters have to absorb. However, most homeowners will agree that it's well worth the trouble. Let's examine some of the principal advantages of owning your own home.

■ Your Own Shelter

As a homeowner, you will enjoy the sense of security that comes with owning and occupying your own home. When you own a single-family house, you are free to do what you like with your property, within the parameters of local zoning restrictions. You can add rooms, change and improve the landscaping, put in a swimming pool or play area, or attach a garage or carport. You can select and install whatever type of roof or windows you prefer, the color of interior and exterior paint, and the style and quality of carpets and drapes. Most important, as a single-family homeowner, you will enjoy an unsurpassed degree of privacy.

For these benefits, you will assume higher expenses for maintenance and take on more risk than renters. You will have to be willing to stay in your house for at least a few years in order to profit from the move, and you will need to maintain your financial stability and a long-term commitment to the community. If these important commitments are kept, the value of your house will increase over time.

If you are among the 13 percent of home buyers who pick a condominium or co-op, you may not be allowed to drastically alter that property to make drastic improvements, at least not without first gaining permission from the association of fellow owners. But then, you are also free from the burdens of property upkeep and can still enjoy a level of security that is not available to renters. Because condos and co-ops most often are located in clusters or in large buildings, many people believe they are too similar in appearance to rental units to justify the investment. However, condos and co-ops today come in such a variety of settings that the market should be investigated before being ruled out.

■ A Sound Investment

Over a long period of time, few investments return as respectable a level of profit as real estate. Investment value should not be the primary reason for buying a home, but over many years the market value will certainly be important to you. Real estate markets are cyclical and regional, meaning that over periods of several years, housing prices will remain stable or perhaps even drop.

In addition, conditions in one region do not necessarily mean the same conditions exist elsewhere. Invariably, different areas of the country experience a wide range of real estate markets at any given time. Over a 30-year period, however, owner-occupied housing has had an impressive track record. During the Great Depression, stock-market values dropped nearly 90 percent while property values dropped only 34 percent. Even during recessions, housing values tend to decline less or even rise in comparison to other investments, and real estate usually outpaces the rate of inflation. According to the Bureau of Labor Statistics and the National Association of Realtors, during the late 1970s (the worst recession since the 1930s), housing values grew between 10 and 15 percent each year. And in the mid-1980s, with inflation running at about 5 percent each year, housing values grew at a higher average rate.

Figure 1.1 summarizes the annual percentage of increases in housing values between 1975 and 1994, and compares that growth rate to increases in the Consumer Price Index (CPI). The illustration of percentage changes is revealing. It shows that housing does exceed inflation, not only now and then, but consistently over time. Buying and keeping a home over many years is a sound investment.

The percentages are only part of the story. Consider how dramatically housing values have increased over the past 30 years. In the decade between 1966 and 1976, the median value of property more than doubled in the United States, from $20,000 to $42,200. The value

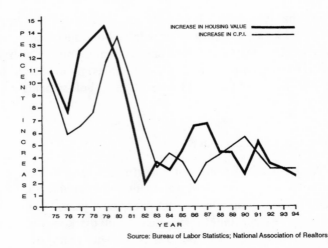

Figure 1.1 Housing Values and Consumer Price Index 1975–94

doubled again over the following 10 years, so that the median value in 1986 was $80,300. Currently, according to the National Association of Realtors, that number has grown to about $110,000. That means that the median value of homes in the United States has grown in 30 years from $20,000 to $110,000, a rate of 550 percent.

Remember, though, that housing values vary drastically from one area to another. The National Association of Realtors analyzes median values overall but also takes into consideration the differences among major geographic regions. Typically, values in the Northeast and West can be twice as much as the values in the Midwest and South. A similar house in San Francisco or New York will cost substantially more than a house in Little Rock or Peoria. A National Association of Home Builders survey showed that the most expensive places to buy property are all in California: San Francisco (median price $285,000); Santa Cruz (median price $215,000); Oxnard/Ventura (median price $195,000); Santa Rosa/Petaluma (median price $182,000); and Salinas/Seaside/ Monterey (median price $169,000).

Usually, housing will increase in value when held for several years, especially in desirable locations, which are limited. Trends in population growth are dictated by the job market, climate, and other social factors, and housing values will vary by region for the same reasons they have varied in the past. The economic health of a region certainly affects housing values. A growing job market brings more people into an area, whereas a declining market has the opposite effect. Interest rates charged by lenders also affect first-time buyers. The lower the interest rate, the greater the number of people who can qualify for loans. Even federal and state income tax rules affect affordability of a home. The deduction of interest is a major factor in affordability because deducting interest expenses reduces the after-tax cost of owning a home.

As in all markets, supply and demand are constantly shifting. When demand increases, construction activity follows. In extreme cases, this leads to excessive building, meaning the supply is greater than the demand. Consequently, prices level out as the market softens. Construction then stops and eventually the process starts all over again. This general trend tends to take between five and seven years but varies considerably by region.

■ Growth in Equity

Looking back to the past is easier than looking forward. The historian is always far more accurate than the futurist. In real estate, it seems that someone is always claiming that values will never grow in the future, that if you haven't bought real estate already, the big opportunity has been missed. Such predictions were made during the mid-1960s through the mid-1990s, when there was a 550 percent rate of growth in housing values.

How can we tell whether or not housing values will grow in the future? The Census Bureau estimates that over the next 60 years, the population of the United States will grow by 50 percent, from the 1992 level of 255 million to 353 million by 2050. All of those people will need a place to live. They will eventually want to share in the American Dream, just as the current population does. It is reasonable to predict that this level of demand will mean housing values will continue to grow in the future as they have in the past. There are no guarantees, but the statistics of the past and projections about the future certainly make a strong case for a good, healthy market.

Your net worth—everything you own, minus everything you owe—will increase over the years you own your home. This growth results from the accumulation of equity in your home. Each payment you make to a lender is divided between principal (payment of the loan balance) and interest. The rate of growth is painfully slow in the early years, when most of the monthly payment consists of interest. But the longer you own your home, the higher the portion of the payment that goes to paying off the debt. The longer you stay in your home, the faster your equity grows.

If you purchase a home for $100,000 and pay off an $80,000 mortgage loan over 30 years, your net worth will increase by $80,000, minus inflation. Above and beyond that, though, your net worth will also grow by the increase in market value of the property. If the home's value increases, your net worth will grow dollar for dollar along with your home's market value.

■ Control over Interest Expense

Home ownership gives you more control over interest expenses, even when the purchase is financed with an adjustable-rate mortgage. With such a contract, the lender can periodically raise the interest rate if other measures of interest rise. The lender is limited, however, in the degree of increase. The limitations are applied each year, as well as overall—meaning that even assuming the worst case, you can predict how expensive it will be to pay for a loan over many years.

The more popular fixed-rate mortgage stabilizes your cost of living. That's because the rate of interest never rises over the entire contractual term, which may be as long as 30 years. So if today's mortgage payment represents 25 percent of your gross pay, it decreases as a percentage each and every time you get a raise. For example, let's assume your family's income is $3,000 per month before taxes and other deductions. Your mortgage payment is $750, which is 25 percent of income. But next year, you get a 5 percent raise, so your income increases to $3,150. Now, that fixed mortgage payment is less than 24 percent of income. If your income rises every year or two, the mortgage payment actually shrinks. Over a period of 30 years, the effect will be significant.

In a very real sense, your payments with a fixed-rate mortgage go down, not up. Renters experience periodic increases in their rent because the landlord's costs (such as property taxes, utilities, insurance, and maintenance) go up. Those costs are invariably passed on to the tenant. If you are a homeowner with a fixed-rate mortgage, inflation actually works for you. Some people describe inflation as the shrink-ing of the dollar, since money's value is eroded as prices rise. How-ever, since the mortgage payment is fixed, the real expense of that payment as a portion of your income is lower as inflation (and your income) go up.

If rates fall after you negotiate a fixed-rate mortgage, you can still cash in by refinancing the loan, and either lower your monthly payment or keep the payment the same but pay off the loan in a shorter time.

■ Improvements Add Value

As you upgrade your home by adding living space or remodeling rooms, the value of your home increases. Any improvements can add value dollar for dollar and sometimes can increase value above and be-yond the cost of those improvements.

The opportunity for you to increase the value of your investment is unmatched by any other form of investment—because improvements can be paid for with borrowed money. By approaching a lender and ap-plying for a home improvement loan, the entire cost of the improve-ment is achieved with the security of home equity. Therefore, the borrowed money is invested back into the home. The interest you pay on the loan is deductible, and the value of the home goes up.

Although borrowing money depletes the present equity in your home, the improvement restores it and the potential for future market value. By paying back the home improvement loan, you further in-crease the home's value, and you and your family enjoy the home more, which is the motivation for undertaking the improvement in the first place.

■ Equity Growth

Your home's value increases with every improvement you make and with each monthly payment (which repays the lender). These are not the only ways that your home's value increases, however. Over time, the value of your property will grow because the demand for housing grows with the population. Over three decades, it is not uncommon to see housing values grow significantly. Not only have housing values kept pace with inflation; in most years those values have surpassed inflation, sometimes by quite a bit.

■ Yearly Tax Benefits

Federal tax rules allow you to deduct the interest paid on mortgage loans you take out to purchase, build, or improve your "primary residence" (the home you live in for most of the year) *and* for a second residence. For most people, that covers all the interest they pay on all of their mortgages. Many states allow the same or similar deductions as well. In today's social debate about tax reform and deficit reduction, the question of continuing to allow mortgage deductions inevitably rises. Some reformers have even suggested limiting the amount of the deduction. Most tax experts agree that completely eliminating the deduction would be detrimental to the housing market in the United States. Two possibilities are most often heard: the limitation of interest in such a way that most first-time buyers would not be affected, and the complete elimination of income taxes, to be replaced with a flat tax or a national sales tax. In theory, doing away with income taxes would result in such a huge improvement in our economy that more people could afford homes, even without the interest deduction.

Until such proposals actually become law, they are nothing more than ideas. As of the publication date of this book, you are allowed to itemize deductions and to write off interest on a first and second home with total mortgages of $1 million or less. For the majority of first-time buyers, that is a comfortable ceiling.

The tax benefit of writing off mortgage interest makes a substantial difference in the tax you will owe to the government at the end of each year, which actually reduces your housing costs. Many people think they cannot afford mortgage payments based on the amount they presently pay for rent, but the comparison should be made on an after-tax basis. Owning and paying for a home might not cost as much as you think.

Since most of the mortgage payments you make during the first few years of home ownership go toward paying off the interest on the mortgage loan, your tax deduction can be sizable. If your marginal tax rate (the rate of the combined federal and state income taxes) is 30 percent, every dollar of itemized deductions reduces your tax liability by 30 percent. For example, let's say your total mortgage interest last year was $9,870. In preparing your state and local tax returns, you discover that your marginal tax rate is 30 percent. When you declare $9,870 as an itemized deduction, your tax liability is reduced by $2,961 ($9,870 x 30 percent). Your after-tax mortgage cost is $6,909 ($9,870 - $2,961).

To further demonstrate this point, look at the total interest costs on a $100,000 loan (with a 30-year repayment term) at 10.5 percent. In the first three years, your total interest expenses are

Year 1	$10,476.36
Year 2	10,421.21
Year 3	10,359.97

If you itemize deductions and write off these expenses, your after-tax interest expenses are

Year 1	$7,333.45
Year 2	7,294.85
Year 3	7,251.98

To what extent home ownership is advantageous compared with renting depends on the individual tax rate and the amount of rent you are paying. Over many years, your interest advantage begins to diminish as a higher portion of your payment goes toward the principal. However, the rate of decline is so gradual that it should not be taken into consideration when comparing owning a home and renting.

Also remember that with a home, you benefit directly from rising real estate prices, and you can fix your housing costs over several years. Renters can claim neither of these benefits. Their costs rise as the landlord's costs rise, and they accumulate no equity as long as they rent.

Here's how to make the comparison. Compare the real after-tax cost of purchasing a home with the actual monthly rent payment. To show how this comparison is made, let's assume your rent is $700 per month. With a 30-year, $100,000 mortgage at 10.5 percent interest, your mortgage payment is $914.74 per month, or $214.74 more than renting. At first glance, this additional monthly payment appears to be significant. But if your marginal tax rate is 30 percent, the actual cost is less than $914.74. Assuming that on average during the first year, monthly interest is about $875, the tax benefit of buying a home is 30 percent of that, or $262.50. In this example, the mortgage payment works out to be $47.56 *less* than the rent payment after taxes are considered:

	Rent	Mortgage
Monthly	$700.00	$914.74
Less: tax benefits (30% of $875)		262.50
After-tax cost	$700.00	$652.24

This example compares costs on the basis of interest only. Realistically, homeowners have other expenses—including property taxes, insurance, utilities, and maintenance—that should also be considered. These costs vary by area. Our point here is to illustrate that, given the many benefits of owning a home, the comparative cost of owning versus renting is far less drastic than many people believe.

■ Other Tax Breaks

In addition to writing off interest, the tax rules allow you to deduct property taxes as well. That's another itemized deduction that helps reduce your real cost of housing.

As a homeowner, you are also allowed to defer market-value gains. No other investment provides you with this feature. If you sell your home at a profit, you do not have to pay taxes on that profit as long as you buy (or build) another home within two years. That rule works as long as the new home costs more than the amount at which the first home was sold. If the new home costs less, only the difference is taxed.

If you are 55 or over, there's another tax break in the federal tax rules. You are entitled to an exclusion of taxes on as much as $125,000 of profit from selling your home. This once-in-a-lifetime tax break should be kept in mind for anyone involved in retirement planning, because it enables you to cash in a home that has grown in value and avoid taxes.

■ Risks

There are risks in home ownership, as there are with all forms of investing. One of the greatest risks is that you won't be able to keep up with the mortgage payments. Another risk is that the value of your property, for whatever economic or social reasons, will not appreciate and might even depreciate.

The first risk, the inability to keep up with payments, is the same risk renters face. In many respects, owning a home is less risky than renting. Most foreclosures result from a buyer purchasing a home far beyond his or her financial capabilities, or financial reverses (such as the loss of a job, disability, divorce, or the death of a wage earner) that suddenly make homeowning unaffordable. Since job loss will jeopardize both owned and rented households—it's one of the risks we all live with—it certainly should not prevent you from planning to buy your own home. Unexpected loss of income due to death or disability can be protected against by the purchase of insurance, so that your investment in a home will not be lost even with the loss in earnings.

As a group, homeowners have managed to keep up with their mortgage payments over time. About 96 percent of all homeowners make their mortgage payment on time every month, which means the delinquency rate averages only 4 percent. Most of those delinquencies are eventually corrected, too. According to the Mortgage Bankers Association of America, only 1 percent of mortgages in the United States are foreclosed each year.

The second risk, depreciation, sometimes cannot be predicted or controlled. However, if you inspect properties carefully and keep abreast of what is going on in your community, you can minimize the risk that your property's value will fall.

As a homeowner, you take on additional responsibilities that renters don't. A house and grounds have to be maintained, both for personal and financial reasons. Proper maintenance adds value to a home, whereas failing to keep a home in good shape reduces its value. As a homeowner, you have to be prepared for the additional expenses that come along with owning your own home. Even if you are fairly handy, some repairs may be too difficult for you to make, and, unlike a renter, you can't call the landlord. As a result, you may have to hire professional help: a plumber, an electrician, a roofer, even a tree surgeon. Since maintenance expenses crop up frequently enough, you have to manage your money with the unexpected in mind in order to make timely repairs while still keeping control of your family budget.

All those repairs and responsibilities are sobering realities. Your lifestyle will change in other ways as well. For example, the annual family vacation might have to be curtailed or even eliminated to pay for a new roof, or you might have to put off buying a new car because your heating system needs overhauling. However, if you have a house thoroughly inspected before you buy it, you should have few unexpected repairs, at least for a few years.

In addition to unexpected bills, there are other expenses involved with owning your own home, for example, utilities are usually higher in a house than in an apartment. If you have a yard, you will also have to pay for lawn and yard maintenance equipment, ladders, and tools. However, if you protect yourself against the risks that come with buying and owning a home, and if you carefully plan ahead, your housing investment will be gratifying and profitable.

■ Supply and Demand

What's on the market and how much people are willing to pay for these homes is the essence of supply and demand. Many factors go into this constantly changing balance of market forces, including:

Interest rates. In the past, interest rates have risen so high that it was nearly impossible for sellers to find buyers for their properties. In the late 1970s, for instance, mortgage interest rates approached 20 percent. When that happens, few would-be buyers can qualify for loans because lenders look at the monthly income of the borrower versus the required monthly payment. If the income-to-payment ratio—set by the lender—is too low, the lender will reject the application.

Under these circumstances, when interest rates are so high that the market freezes up, the rate of interest affects home sales more than the actual market price. If the buyer can find a way to borrow the money, the price of the home becomes secondary and, in some cases, does not even matter. Financing terms alone may dictate whether such properties sell at all, with real estate agents lending their expertise at putting together financing deals for the buyer.

Since those troubled times of distorted inflation, interest rates have been fairly stable and remained within a narrow range. Today, more people can afford to buy homes, some for the first time, because interest rates have not jumped the way they did in the 1970s.

Population. When the number of people looking for housing exceeds the number of houses available, prices have to rise. Demand is higher than the supply. To meet this demand, more construction is undertaken and more homes are made available. This is how the condominium and co-op market grew.

Population trends shift, just as interest rates do, resulting in changes in the supply and demand cycle. One of the factors that created such a tremendous demand for housing during the 1970s was the coming of home-buying age (between 25 and 35) for baby boomers.

Cost of construction. When construction costs rise, including both material and labor, housing prices have to follow. Higher building prices inevitably mean higher costs for home buyers. Builders have to charge more for their work, or sacrifice quality and build homes with cheaper materials or less craftsmanship.

Most people believe that higher home prices can be blamed exclusively on rising construction costs. In reality, the cost of land has to be considered as well. Residential land value increases as the availability of land for development decreases. As cities grow, the need to house new arrivals drives real estate prices up. In some areas, it is the cost of land that affects housing prices more than construction costs.

Availability of financing. Just as changes in interest rates affect people's ability to buy homes, the amount of money available to lend affects the price of homes. The federal government and its mortgage programs play an important role in this process, through the Government National Mortgage Association, the Federal Home Loan Mortgage Corporation, and the Federal Housing Administration. These agencies work with banks and mortgage companies in creating and transferring capital used to finance home purchases.

The policies of private lenders have an impact as well, and those policies vary depending on the money supply. As a lender's money supply is restricted, home buyers are affected directly. Lenders are in the business of making the most profitable loans possible. That means, at times, that mortgage loans are not as competitive as other types of loans the bank could make.

Employment opportunities. In any area, at any given time, the job market directly influences the supply and demand cycle and the price of homes. If large employers are laying off their workers and people want to sell and leave the area, the inventory of homes for sale will grow rapidly, meaning more competition for an ever-shrinking number of buyers. In the opposite scenario, when employers are hiring and cannot find enough local people to fill openings, people from elsewhere will move to the area to find employment. This will create a higher demand for a limited number of homes. As a result, home prices will be forced up.

Supply. A supply surplus will cause new construction to stop (because there are too many homes on the market and a shortage of buyers), and a demand surplus will cause new home construction to explode (because demand is high and there are not enough homes). And at any point in the cycle, these conditions can reverse. The cycle is dynamic. It does not remain the same for any length of time but is constantly moving as supply and demand vary.

To determine whether a community is experiencing a high-supply or high-demand situation, look at the number of available homes, and compare it with the number of homes available in the recent past. This information can be obtained, in most areas, from a Multiple Listing Service (MLS). Any real estate agent who is a member of MLS can advise you about the trends.

Since a home is a sound investment, you can probably expect to make a profit when you sell it. However, the timing of your sale will determine not only how much profit you make, but also how long it will take to find a buyer. Remember, too, that once you sell your home, you will need to buy a home again (unless you choose to rent). Even if you make a profit selling your home, chances are that that money will be used to purchase a new home. You can, of course, sell your high-priced home and buy a home in a part of the country where market prices are lower.

When buying a home, try not to think like a speculator. Buy a home because you want to live there for many years, not because you think the value of the property will increase. Rapid growth in property values is unusual; don't count on it (the market varies depending on where you live). Consider your home as a personal investment that you will have for many years. Do not expect to realize a quick profit within a short time, because that is unlikely to happen.

2

Alternatives to Owning a Home

The decision to buy a home should not be made lightly. Some people are tempted by books and seminars that promise untold riches in real estate and shamelessly promote complex schemes that can make anyone a millionaire, "no money down."

The reality is this: Real estate is a serious investment that requires a commitment—personal as well as financial—on your part. It could be the largest purchase you'll make in your lifetime. A down payment is only the beginning; ownership involves ongoing mortgage and tax payments as well as the expense of maintenance and improvements. Also, real estate doesn't mysteriously appreciate. The housing market determines its value.

If you buy before you are able to afford a home, you will probably regret the decision. You might be forced to sell at a loss or, worse, you might have to default on your mortgage loan. As a consequence, you might lose your entire down payment and suffer a poor credit rating. If that occurs, your chances of getting a new loan in the future will be very slim, even when you become financially solvent and in a better position to buy.

Put off buying a home if

- Your income is too low; you can't afford mortgage payments that are substantially higher than what you currently pay in rent.

- You're not sure you want to remain in the area, or are unable to, because of the job market or other conditions. Recognize that you might have to move a few times before you'll be ready to settle down in one community.
- Your job or occupation makes it difficult for you to stay in one area for long. If there's a chance your employer will transfer you elsewhere, especially if that could occur at frequent intervals, it might not make sense to buy a home yet.
- Financial freedom is a high priority for you, so you're not willing to tie up investment capital in a home. Home buyers should be prepared to settle down and stay in one place for a while, and be willing to invest their money in a down payment.

You are a good candidate to buy a home if

- You have a steady income adequate to qualify for financing.
- Your marginal tax rate is high enough that interest deductions are valuable.
- You are reasonably certain you will stay in the community for the next few years.
- You don't expect to be transferred to another job location, or you are in a position in which you could decline to take a transfer.
- You are willing and ready to make the commitment required to buy a home.

Buying a home is not a small commitment. On average, mortgages and other costs of housing account for 20 percent of a home buyer's income. For renters, the average amount spent on housing is about 30 percent. A good part of that difference is due to marital status. About two-thirds of homeowners are married, but only one-third of renters are married. As a result, the income of homeowners is about double the income of renters.

Age is an important factor in determining who buys homes. In general, younger people do not earn as much income per month because they do not have the experience to command higher salaries. Better pay comes with having more experience. Therefore, the younger you are, the more difficult it will be to qualify for a home loan.

The good news is that the majority of people eventually buy their own homes. The more years you have under your belt, the more likely it is that you will become part of the homeowner majority. The following are the rates of ownership, according to the U.S. Bureau of the Census, broken down by age groups:

Age Range	% Owning a Home
under 25	15
25–29	34
30–34	51
35–39	62
40–44	69
45–49	74
50–54	77
55–59	79
60–64	81
65–69	81
70–74	80
75 or older	73

From these statistics, you can see that by the time you're in your sixties, there's a four out of five chance that you will own your own home. After that age, the numbers start to fall off as people sell their homes and move to lower-maintenance apartments, to retirement homes, or to the homes of relatives.

▪ Risk

Both the decision to buy and the decision to delay involve risk. If you are ready to buy but wait, you face the possibility that interest rates might be higher in the future, meaning it will be more difficult to qualify for a loan *and* more expensive to pay off a mortgage. For example, on a $100,000 30-year loan, the difference in the monthly payment from one percentage point to another is about $75 per month. That might not seem like much, but when you multiply it by 30 years, it comes out to about $27,000.

In addition, housing prices might increase while you are waiting to buy. In some markets, they might skyrocket. Between 1987 and 1989, home prices in some parts of California doubled. Such occurrences are difficult to predict.

For every year you delay, you extend the length of your repayment terms by a year. If you're 35 and you finance a home over 30 years, it will be paid off by the time you reach 65. But if you wait until you're 40, you won't pay off that 30-year mortgage until you are 70.

However, it makes sense to delay in some situations. For example, if you are uncertain about your career, buying a home could be a costly mistake. You may decide to pursue a career that will require you to move. If you own a home and the market is soft (meaning the demand for homes is so low that it will be difficult to sell)—it could mean missing a career opportunity.

It would also be a mistake to purchase a home if you are having marital problems. Divorces are complicated and painful enough without having to decide how a mortgaged home will be paid for or how the proceeds of the sale will be divided. It could spell financial disaster for both husband and wife.

Some people are not ready to buy a home because they're simply not ready to live in one place for a long period of time. Many Americans like to uproot themselves every few years and move to new areas, effectively starting over. Most eventually settle down, but for some people that takes longer than for others. If you are nomadic, you should decide where you want to live before you buy a home.

■ Being a Renter

For some people, there are advantages to renting. Rents in many areas do not increase as quickly as house prices. Typically, that occurs when the market for home ownership is soft, and a large number of rental houses or apartments are available. This availability is due to the fact that most people, given the choice, would prefer to own a home rather than rent. The issues of privacy, control, financial security, and profit all make home ownership desirable. These factors hold down the market for rentals. As a result, rental increases do not keep pace with housing prices.

This explains why some people prefer to remain renters, especially those expecting to move. (Renters tend to move more than homeowners, if only because selling a house and buying another is far more complicated than just finding another apartment.) In addition, apartment dwellers usually have lower utility bills because the landlord pays some of these costs. Utilities also cost less for people living in smaller apartments than for people living in larger homes.

Renters do live with considerable disadvantages, though. The greatest one is that rents can and do rise unexpectedly and, in some cases, they rise precipitously. If there are too few rental units to meet the demand, rents invariably will go up. This is another example of the supply and demand cycle. Another disadvantage for renters is that they might not be able to keep their rental units for as long as they would like. The owner might sell the building to someone else, and increased rents may result; or the units may be converted to co-ops or condominiums, forcing renters to buy their apartments or move on.

Apartment renters live very close to their neighbors. This makes the renting lifestyle much different from the homeowner lifestyle. There is a greater obligation for the renter and for all the renting neighbors to be considerate of those people who live above, below, and on either side of them. Renters who have to put up with noisy or inconsiderate neighbors may find life to be unbearable, and possibly confrontational.

Renters depend on a manager or landlord for building maintenance. The signs of a poorly run apartment complex are visible both inside the apartment and outside—in the garden area, the parking lot, and the building entrance. Some owners are not willing to invest money to keep their property in good shape, which means renters have to suffer deferred maintenance problems and the resulting hazards. Homeowners have greater control of living conditions that affect their quality of life. For anyone who has had to live in a poorly maintained apartment, that benefit of home ownership is probably the most appealing.

The decision to buy or to rent also depends on where you want to live. For a city dweller, renting might be less expensive than buying, even considering the tax benefits of home ownership. Many urban apartment renters don't need to own a car, do yard work, pay long-distance commuting bills, or be concerned with home maintenance.

■ Renting with an Option to Buy

Renters who want to buy a home but lack the cash for a down payment might be able to purchase it by renting with an option to buy. This arrangement, which is also known as a lease option, depends on the current owner's willingness to enter into an agreement and became popular during those years when interest rates were too high and many sellers found it to be the only way to attract a buyer.

With the typical option-to-buy contract, you become a tenant and enter into a lease arrangement with the owner. You agree to pay a monthly amount that represents part rent and part accumulated down payment, to be applied to the purchase price at a later date. The down payment is usually refundable if you do *not* exercise the option by a specified deadline. The purchase price is fixed and the owner agrees to sell you the home at that price, even if the value of the property changes after you purchase it. A popular lease term for this arrangement is three years.

For example, let's say you want to buy a house that presently rents for $700 per month. You agree to make monthly payments of $950, with $250 applied toward a down payment. Within 36 months, you accumulate $9,000, which is equal to 10 percent of the agreed sales price, $90,000. As part of the deal, the owner agrees that, upon exercise of the option, he or she will get a second mortgage on the house for $9,000. You will have to finance 80 percent of the purchase price through a lender:

Accumulated down payment	$ 9,000
Second mortgage from seller	9,000
Financed, 80%	<u>72,000</u>
Total	$90,000

The amount of the deposit required for an option-to-buy contract varies depending on the amount of the rent, the asking price of the home, and the time allowed for accumulation of a down payment *and* for exercising the option. Remember, if you do not exercise the option by the agreed-upon deadline, it expires. The option itself has a dollar value, and these deals sometimes involve paying for the option. For example, in return for fixing the price of the house at $90,000, you might be asked to pay a nonrefundable fee of $1,000 (or more).

Being able to fix the price of a home is an important feature of the option-to-buy contract, as it protects you in the event of unexpected increases in market value. For example, suppose you enter into an option-to-buy contract to purchase a home for $90,000 within 36 months, but at the end of that term the home is worth $150,000? Because you have an agreement, the seller is obligated to sell the home to you for the contracted price of $90,000.

For some people, an option-to-buy contract is the most practical way to buy a house and, in some cases, the only way. The trade-off is that you will likely pay higher rent than the market rent value, in exchange for the option. The value of the arrangement is that it ensures you a fixed purchase price and allows time for accumulation of a down payment.

The option-to-buy contract should clearly spell out all of the terms of the agreement, including the date the option expires, how option money will be handled (for example, will it be put into a special account where interest can accumulate?), what will happen if you do not exercise the option, and all other terms. In some contracts, return of the deposit money might be contingent on the seller's finding another buyer for the property. If the seller were to enter into an option-to-buy contract with someone else, it is conceivable that your deposit money could remain tied up for years. Be sure all the possible outcomes are defined in the contract and that all terms are clear.

In addition, the agreement should be recorded with your local recorder or assessor's office. The option-to-buy contract is an obligation on the property, and recording it protects you in the event the seller decides to sell or refinance the property without telling you. Before you enter into an option-to-buy contract, you should consult with an attorney and have the attorney review the proposed terms before you sign the agreement.

3

The Question of Affordability

What can I afford? is the most basic and most pressing question for most first-time home buyers. You can't buy a home if you can't afford the down payment or the monthly payments. Unfortunately, homes in some areas of the country are priced so high as to be unaffordable. The down payments required in these markets are staggering, the monthly payments beyond the average person's ability to pay, and even qualifying for loans is beyond the reach of most people. Such homes are practical only for people coming to the table with large down payments or equity in a previously owned home.

The first thing a prospective home buyer needs to do is to identify the right markets. That often means finding neighborhoods with homes priced at the low end of the scale—but not "run-down" homes, fixer-uppers, or homes in crime-prone areas. Many older, established neighborhoods have modestly priced homes that will work well for the first-time buyer.

To save money for a down payment, start by putting yourself on a budget. Explore financing options that will help you get a home with a minimum down payment. The day may come when you will be able to afford that Tudor mansion of your dreams, but until then, approach the housing market as a well-informed buyer with realistic expectations.

According to the Chicago Title Insurance Company, the average down payment paid by first-time buyers is 14 to 15 percent of the purchase price. However, that percentage is declining slightly each year.

■ Calculating a Home's Affordability

1. The first step in determining whether you can afford to buy a home is to figure out how much down payment will be required for the typical home in your area. If you were to pay 14.5 percent of the purchase price, how much down payment would you need? The following are some examples:

Purchase Price	Down Payment
$ 50,000	$ 7,250
75,000	10,875
100,000	14,500
125,000	18,125
150,000	21,750
175,000	25,375
200,000	29,000
225,000	32,625
250,000	36,250

2. Set a standard based on what you can afford to buy, based on your annual income. You might decide that a house should cost no more than two and one-half times your gross annual income, as in the following examples:

Annual Income	Maximum Price
$ 20,000	$ 50,000
30,000	75,000
40,000	100,000
50,000	125,000
60,000	150,000
70,000	175,000
80,000	200,000
90,000	225,000
100,000	250,000

3. Be willing to settle for less than your dream home, if necessary. Setting too high a standard will mean being disappointed. If you are expecting to get a top-of-the-line home with the highest quality construction the first time out, you might not be able to afford it. An older, smaller, more modestly constructed home may satisfy your needs and serve as a good starter home.

4. Decide on the best financing strategies. For example, if you have a large amount of cash available for a down payment, should you use it all or just pay the minimum? A larger down payment means less overall interest expense and lower monthly payments, but keeping a cash reserve means you'll have more financial security in the event of an emergency.

5. If you don't have much money available, start a savings plan and stick to the plan. In a few years, even a fairly modest savings account can grow to a sum large enough for a down payment.

6. Recognize the fact that the younger you are when you buy, the more time you will have to pay off a mortgage loan before you reach retirement. According to the Chicago Title Insurance Company, the average age of first-time home buyers is around 31 but is gradually rising.

7. After you analyze your average income, the housing prices in the area, and how much you will need for a down payment, you should be able to determine how much you can afford to pay each month. Find out about home price information in your area (you can call the *Consumer Reports* Home Price Service at 1-800-775-1212) and ask a lender if you qualify for a mortgage loan. If you do, the lender can help you figure out the monthly payment you will need to make. Typically, first-time buyers pay between $1,000 and $1,100 per month in mortgage payments.

Some first-time buyers realize that in order to afford that first home and qualify for a loan, a larger down payment will be needed. If you need to save for that down payment, avoid the three most common mistakes families make when they try to start a savings plan:

- Don't save only what's left over from a paycheck after basic expenses have been paid. Instead, make your savings contribution every month *before* distributing the rest of the money to your budget. Include savings as a regular expense at the top of your priority list and invest it first, without exception.

- Don't set an unrealistic budget. Don't expect to save more money each month than you can actually afford. Unexpected expenses are inevitable, and you need to allow some room in your budget for those expenses. A savings plan won't work unless it's practical.
- Don't misuse credit. Avoid using credit cards or taking out bank loans unless it's absolutely essential. If you have to make regular monthly payments to pay off credit debts, it will be that much harder to save for a down payment on a house. Every dollar you spend paying off unnecessary debts is a dollar *not* saved.

Once you are ready to buy, plan to look for a home in the off season. Avoid spring and early summer, the "jump" months, when most buyers begin looking for homes. During those months, sellers have more buyers to choose from, giving them a market advantage.

■ Tax Considerations

The "real" cost of buying a home—that is, the cost after deductions on your federal and state tax returns have been taken into account—should also be looked at to determine affordability. You can't compare renting to buying if tax deductions are not factored into the comparison. The difference between after-tax mortgage payments and rent payments might be less than you think, especially if you pay state tax as well as federal tax.

When comparing costs, remember that whereas deductions will be significant in the early years, they do decline over time. But the yearly decline is slight. With a 10 percent mortgage paid over 30 years, approximately 9 percent of the loan will be paid off after the tenth year. This means that with a starting loan balance of $80,000, you will still owe about $72,750 after 10 years, even though you will have paid $84,250. The majority of the money paid early in the life of the mortgage loan goes toward paying off the interest. The ratio between principal and interest, however, diminishes over time at an ever-increasing rate, so that interest is eventually only a small portion of the total payment. (Interest is computed each month based on the outstanding loan balance, so the higher that balance, the higher the interest.) But it is not until the 22nd or 23rd year of a 30-year term that more than half of the total payment actually goes toward principal.

■ Defining "Affordable"

As your income rises over the years, the cost of housing becomes less of a burden, since mortgage costs can be fixed (with a fixed-rate mortgage) or controlled (limited by rate ceilings in adjustable-rate mortgage contracts). In other words, with time, housing is not only a sound investment with growing values, but one that should become less of a financial burden as well.

The growing equity in a home is another matter to consider. It represents tax-free money that you can borrow for improvements (which can further increase the value of your home), or to make other investments, or that can be used to make a larger down payment on a more expensive home you might want to buy in the future.

If you have a large sum of money for a down payment, you can afford to look at a wider range of homes than if you have little or no money. Remember, though, that you will still have to qualify for a mortgage loan. Even if you can afford to put down 20 percent of the purchase price, you might not qualify for financing because your income may not meet the lender's requirements. In addition to the down payment, you also need enough money to cover closing costs, which could add up to thousands of dollars.

When shopping for financing, be aware that a real bargain is a fair and competitive rate based on the current market. Be wary of any deal that sounds too good. Read the fine print. And don't fall for "creative financing" schemes, which are usually no more than clever advertising tricks and attention-getting offers. What sounds like a good deal could lead to financial trouble and higher costs than you expected. Be thorough in your search for financing.

When buying your first home, strike a balance between current affordability and future marketability. Decide if you want to invest in a home that is larger than what you need. A large home with a good location and a comfortable floor plan will be more marketable when you decide to sell, and will also be more likely to appreciate in value. Consider the features that can add or detract from the value of a home. Be aware, for example, that houses on busy streets—which are priced to sell—will not appreciate as well as houses on quieter streets. Therefore, today's bargain could be tomorrow's less-desirable home. In short, try to view homes not only with a buyer's eye, but also with a seller's more critical eye.

One good way to evaluate a home is to think in terms of what your family's minimum requirements for living space will be for the next five years. Planning beyond that is not practical, since needs can change as a result of unforeseen circumstances. Moreover, if your primary concern is being able to afford a first home, there is no point in thinking of a long-term commitment.

■ Some Buying Considerations

Location. This is probably the single most important consideration to keep in mind when buying a home. In the real estate business, it is said that three things count in establishing property value: location, location, location. Houses may be updated, renovated, and improved, but neighborhoods and communities tend to retain their basic character and market value over periods of time. Is the home in a safe neighborhood where people want to move, buy homes, and raise families? Is there access to schools, transportation, and shopping? Is the area run-down, filled with high crime, or noisy? Are people moving away to better places to live? Look for an area where homes sell quickly and easily. It's a good sign if houses stay on the market for less than three months; if it takes six months or more for homes to sell, look elsewhere. Avoid neighborhoods with a large number of undeveloped lots, abandoned homes, poorly maintained homes and yards, a large number of FOR SALE signs, or with mixed zoning (commercial and residential together).

Estate building. Buying a home is an important step in building your estate. For most Americans, it is the largest investment they will ever make. In addition to buying a home for shelter, you want to maximize its investment value by selecting a home in a good neighborhood.

Community interest. Do you truly like the city or town where the neighborhood is located? Or are you looking at neighborhoods just because of affordability, without really thinking about living there? The selection of a community is important not only based on how much homes cost in that community but also how much you will enjoy living there.

Children's ages. What are your children's ages and are the characteristics of the neighborhood a good match for your children? Are there other children in the same age range? Consider the character and demographics of an area with your children in mind.

Appearance. In order for a home to be a good investment, it should be conservative in design and attractive at first glance. Unusually shaped windows or roof slant, oddly-shaped rooms, and poor layout all detract from the resalability of a home. A good investment home fits in with other homes in the immediate area. For example, an exceptionally large home will be limited in value if it does not conform to the size of the other homes in that neighborhood.

Your career. When deciding where you want to live, your career will undoubtedly play a part in the decision. Can you find work in your chosen field in the area? Or are you likely to be transferred or forced to move to find a job in the future?

Living space. Look for a home that was planned for the comfort of its occupants. Convenience and utility are important. The floor plan should be intelligent, logical, and natural, providing easy flow from one part of the house to another. It also means the house should not be overly expensive to heat or cool.

Expansion potential. Can a room be added on easily? Is the yard large enough so that a first-floor addition can be built without violating local building codes and zoning laws? Can a second story be added without making major changes in the foundation or radically changing the house's appearance?

Room size. Are the rooms comfortably sized? Buyers will be discouraged if kitchens and bathrooms are too small and poorly equipped. Basic and popular combinations of features—such as three bedrooms and two bathrooms—make homes more marketable. Conformity is an important feature in the housing market. People expect certain features and do not want to do without them.

4

Working with an Agent

The ideal home is one that meets your needs, is within a price range you can afford, and is located in an area where you want to live. But since any number of homes may fit that description, it would be a formidable task to view all potentially suitable homes.

You can find a home through word of mouth or newspaper advertisements, or by driving around an area you like and looking for FOR SALE signs. However, most people seek out a real estate agent.

■ The Real Estate Agent

When you work with an agent—or any other professional—begin by setting a standard for yourself. No matter what advice you get, make your own decisions. An agent's professional, informed opinion can be valuable, but it is not prudent to defer your decision on which home to buy to the agent.

To understand the relationship between the real estate agent, the seller, and the buyer, the meaning of the word "agency" needs to be defined. Whenever one person is given the authority to act on behalf of someone else, that is described as an agency relationship. The *agent* is given these rights by the *principal* (usually the seller) to facilitate the real estate transaction.

A real estate *broker* matches sellers and buyers in a real estate deal. When a homeowner wants to sell, the broker is retained to act as agent for the seller. The seller, who is the principal, depends on the agent to locate a buyer. In other words, the broker (or a broker's agent) is working for the seller, not the buyer.

The broker is paid a commission for finding a buyer, and in most arrangements that commission is paid by the seller. As a buyer, you are entitled to fair treatment during the real estate transaction, but you would be wise to remember that the broker works for the seller, not you.

Even though most brokers will take every measure to treat the buyer fairly, you should never forget they have a legal obligation to the seller. As the old saying goes, "Let the buyer beware."

Brokers hire any number of people to carry out transactions in their name. Although brokers carry a direct liability for anything said or done in their name, some agents or salespeople may operate beyond their authority. Be aware of agents who give tax or financial advice, or who say that they are giving you confidential information.

Some of the titles used by real estate agents can be confusing to the novice home buyer. A *realtor* is a member of a local real estate board affiliated with the National Association of Realtors, the national association that tests and certifies its members and also publishes a code of professional ethics. Salespeople working for a realtor are sometimes called realtor-associates, which is also a designation assigned after they pass an examination. We'll call the salesperson an agent for the rest of this chapter. That's the person you're most likely to deal with. He or she works for the broker, who owns the brokerage firm.

As a buyer you are a customer, but you do not share directly in the agency relationship. However, an agent does have an obligation to show you available homes in the price range and neighborhoods you specify.

Purchasers are entitled to disclosure by the agent, especially about possible or known defects in a property. In many court cases, real estate buyers have succeeded in gaining awards against agents by proving that some important information was misrepresented by the agent. The courts have established that agents or brokers must disclose "material facts" to purchasers, *and* that they are even responsible for information that may not have been known at the time of the transaction. If the agent should have known the information, he or she can be held liable.

This trend—for courts to hold brokers and agents liable for disclosure to purchasers—has led to important changes in brokerage policies. First, many brokerage firms now supply purchasers with written disclosure about the agency's status. A brokerage firm may actually encourage purchasers to hire a buyer's agent to protect the purchaser's interests. The written disclosure spells out the agency's role in the transaction. It states that the agency is working for the seller and is paid by the seller. For a buyer, this is essential information. However, it is only one form of disclosure. The brokerage firm may also protect itself from liability by ensuring that documented home inspections are performed. The agency's position is full of liability. The courts have ruled that agencies may be held responsible even for undisclosed defects in cases where they should have known about the defects, or should have disclosed them.

Because the listing and selling brokers are both paid by the seller, the buyer may be entirely unrepresented. Having a buyer's agent in the picture ensures that both parties are at least represented by a professional. But even that does not necessarily satisfy the need for discovery and disclosure of defects. A more practical trend is to require a paid-for professional home inspection as part of the contract. That protects everyone and also reveals any real defects, large or small.

■ What to Look out For

Avoid agents or brokers who exhibit any of the following characteristics:

- You are constantly shown homes *above* your maximum range, even after you have specifically told the agent what you can afford. If you have set your sights far below what is available, the agent cannot show you anything. But if there are homes in your price range and the agent will not show them to you, stop wasting your time. Find a more responsive agent.
- You specify what kind of neighborhood, house size, and number of rooms you want, but the agent shows you homes that don't meet your requests. This probably means the agent doesn't have what you're looking for. The agent should be willing to show you other agents' listings as well.

- The agency is not a member of the local Multiple Listing Service (MLS). The majority of homes on the market are transacted through the MLS, so most serious agencies are members. Not belonging to the MLS could be a sign that the agency has had compliance problems and is under suspension.
- The agent is not licensed. This is usually a violation of state law, and indicates that you are not protected under the law in the event of a dispute with that agent.
- The agent gives you confidential information he or she has supposedly gotten from the seller or another agent. This is unprofessional conduct and, in most cases, the information is false. It is a sales technique designed to earn your trust. You should not trust an agent who relies on this kind of manipulation.
- The agent tries to tell you what you want, arguing with you when you say you want something else. *You* are the expert in knowing what you want. A professional agent should respect your needs and make an effort to find you what you want.
- The agent offers you tax, financial, or legal advice. Real estate agents are licensed to do only one thing: bring together a buyer and a seller.
- The agent argues with you concerning an offer you want to make on a home. It is the agent's responsibility to communicate all serious offers to the seller, even if that means they will earn a lower commission. If the agent believes your offer is unreasonably low, he or she should discuss the problem with you; but if you are determined to make the offer, insist that the agent follow through.

You have the right to work with any agent you want. As a buyer, you normally will not enter into a contractual agreement with the agent as the seller does. Therefore, if you are unhappy or uneasy with an agent or their selling techniques or personal style, switch to someone else. If the agent is unresponsive and does not show you the types of properties you want to see, find a new agent. Even if an agent has spent a lot of time showing you homes, you are under no obligation to work with that agent exclusively.

If you do find someone who works hard for you and responds to your needs, it is a good sign. With the MLS system set up the way it is, any member agent is free to show any listed property to you, so an agency is no better than another just because it has more agents or more listings. In fact you might get more personalized service working with a smaller agency. The major benefit of larger agencies is greater contact between agents and their clients.

A word of caution: If you are shown a property by one agent and, a few weeks later, another agent shows you the same property and you end up buying it, the first agent will probably want a commission—even if you were dissatisfied with their service and stopped working with them. However, as the buyer, you are under no obligation to decide who gets what. It is a problem the brokers should straighten out between themselves. As a courtesy, however, you should advise your agent if he or she shows you a property that another agent has already shown you.

■ Buyer's Agents

Buyers can hire their own representatives—a buyer's agent—to find a home for them. Such an agent will want a set fee for locating a suitable property. This is a common practice in commercial real estate and might be worth considering if you want a broker to work exclusively for you.

Hiring a buyer's agent has its drawbacks. It's always better for prospective home buyers to check out the whole market. Whereas a buyer's agent might work hard for you, the relationship tends to limit the search. However, if you end up making an offer on a property for which your selling agent is not also the listing agent, you can ask your

• •

A Warning

Never allow yourself to be bullied into signing a real estate contract, and never write a check unless all the terms of the deal are put in writing. In a real estate contract, verbal promises and warranties do not count; everything has to be in the contract. Always take the time to consider every property carefully, and compare similar properties in your decision-making process. Don't make a decision under pressure; if you miss a great deal, there will be other opportunities. Make a sensible offer according to your evaluation, at what you believe to be a fair price for the home.

• •

agent to specify on the real estate contract that he or she is acting as the buyer's agent; the listing agent will be in the position of the seller's agent, and everyone will be represented. If you are comfortable with your agent, this alternative works out well and costs you nothing extra.

■ Buying Without an Agent

Should you negotiate your own contract for a home, without an agent's help? Some people reason that they are in a better bargaining position because the seller does not have to pay a sales commission. Most beginning buyers, however, feel considerable apprehension about going through the buying process and negotiating all of the terms without an agent's guidance.

Agents can and do offer valuable guidance to first-time buyers. However, since the use of an escrow company or a real estate attorney is required for a closing, you may be able to receive enough guidance from other sources. Chances are, once the contract is signed, the agent's involvement will be minimal.

You will certainly find some bargain prices in the For Sale By Owner (FSBO) market. However, if you do go that route, don't make the mistake of overlooking the need for professional help: appraisers, pest control inspectors, home inspectors, and an attorney.

Look for a seller who is conscientious and prepared. He or she should supply you with a fact sheet detailing the specifics of the house: the asking price, number of rooms, square footage, whether or not any of the financing can be assumed, type of heating system, age of the roof and internal systems, what appliances or fixtures are included (if any), the age of the house, and other useful information. By supplying this information, the owner demonstrates that he or she is serious and is not just "testing the market."

Many people who try to sell their own homes lose potential buyers because they are overly anxious, too aggressive, or inflexible on the selling price and terms of the sale. They might also forget to mention important features of the home that might have strong appeal. In other words, they are not professional salespeople; they may be too involved with the property to objectively market it.

Ask the seller if they are willing to have the contract reviewed by your attorney. If the seller is not agreeable to this idea, look elsewhere.

Don't try to negotiate with a seller who doesn't want your legal adviser involved in the deal. If you are serious about buying a home and you want to have an appraisal and inspection done at your own cost, the seller should be cooperative. If the seller resists for any reason, or insists on an "as is" sale, that's a danger signal. In addition, if the seller volunteers to carry financing for you so that you won't have to go to the bank, this could be a trap, too. It often means that the house does not qualify for financing for some reason. For example, in some areas to qualify for financing, lenders insist on a concrete foundation rather than post and beam. The seller's offer to carry financing is attractive, but it might indicate some structural problems that will be expensive to correct later, when *you* become the seller.

Expect prompt and cooperative answers to all of your questions when dealing directly with a seller. If the seller is evasive, take that to mean there is a problem. There may be something about the property that the seller does not want to reveal. Be sure you check out the property to your own satisfaction—including a visit to the local planning department to see whether any code violations have been filed against the property, or whether a zoning change is pending in the area.

5

How to Evaluate Locations

On average, first-time buyers in this country stay in their initial homes for less than five years. But no matter how often they move, the most important criterion in choosing a new home remains the same: location, location, location. This is as true today as it ever was, and is reflected in the much higher prices paid for houses on desirable streets and in the more prestigious parts of town.

If you're looking for a home and already have a particular location in mind, you have a good starting point. The following are a few basic criteria for selecting one community over another:

Tax base. Where do the tax dollars come from in that location, and where are those dollars spent? In other words, what do the residents get for the taxes they pay? In many regions, property taxes are the principal source of revenue, so there is more dependence on revenues from that source than in other areas. In comparison, towns with exceptionally large numbers of industrial and commercial tracts are supported by those concerns, which helps to keep residential property taxes down. Do some research on your own at the local assessor's or treasurer's office. Check out the tax situation, including any recent or planned assessments or newly created taxing districts. Look into the needs of the school system, zoning changes affecting real estate development, the condition of town buildings and equipment, and any recent cutbacks in services. It would be wise to visit the local library and check the past year's newspaper coverage of civic issues (if you haven't lived in the area), so you will be up to date on the important issues that might affect your current and future property taxes.

Schools. A large percentage of first-time home buyers have young children or are buying because they want to start a family. Accordingly, the quality of local public schools is of prime importance in choosing a location. Schools are important indicators even for single people or for married couples without children. The quality of the schools will affect your property taxes as well as future property values, including the desirability of your home to a future buyer. Schools, more than any other element, affect every homeowner's property taxes. Ask how students have performed on national tests compared with overall averages. Have the school systems won any awards for quality? Try to get a sense of whether public schools are better or worse than average.

Services. Many well-established communities provide all or most of the basic services: garbage pickup, water and sewer, social and library services, fire and police protection. But some don't, and residents end up paying for private services or living with substandard coverage. For example, an outlying area depending on a county sheriff for police protection may have virtually no emergency protection. Check on living conditions in the area where you want to buy a home, and ask yourself how these conditions will affect your quality of life and the value of the property. Find out whether roads are plowed after a snowfall; the extent of police or sheriff protection including typical response times; and whether the fire department is staffed with full-time or volunteer fire fighters.

Accessibility. Few people are happy with a commute longer than one hour. However, many people living in the suburbs put up with long commutes to work. Good access to the workplace determines property value, and communities in close proximity to places where jobs are located rank high in desirability and price. Proximity to commuter rail lines, buses, and highways is a necessity and a big advantage.

Recreation. Some, but not all, buyers are interested in proximity to areas of recreation: golf courses, public gyms, tennis courts, swimming pools, parks, and ball fields. Families with children will be especially interested in the availability of local facilities.

You should also check statistics on home sales in the area during the past year. Find out what are the asking prices and selling prices of several homes. Check the "swing" (the difference) between these two prices. You can get these statistics from any real estate agent or banker subscribing to the Multiple Listing Service or similar organization. Compare sales for the past year and compute the swing. As a rule, a stable and, hence, desirable neighborhood should experience a swing of 5 percent or less.

If the swing is greater than 5 percent, it can mean one of three things. First, homes are overpriced. Second, there is a shortage of interested buyers in the area. Or third, the market is in a state of flux. That can be good or bad, depending on whether the swing is shrinking or growing. The swing test can also point to faults in homes built by one developer that have very low resale values. Recurrent flooding, mud slides, substandard construction, and similar problems can all affect the swing in a given location.

Next, check how many homes were sold over the past year. This helps you to estimate whether the neighborhood is becoming more desirable or less desirable. If it seems that the number of homes going on the market is on the rise, it could be an indication of problems. Also, compare the inventory of available homes at the beginning of the most recent year and at the end of that year. If that number is currently higher than in the past, the neighborhood might be declining in popularity.

Find out the average time it takes to sell a home. In the most desirable neighborhoods, homes will sell in three months or less. Steer clear of locations where homes remain on the market for more than six months. All of the statistical information you need to evaluate a location is available from a local real estate brokerage firm.

■ Sources of Information

The following people, associations, or resources can be invaluable in assisting you in your investigation of the local housing market.

Real estate agents. Ask several agents which areas of the city or town are the best maintained. Keep in mind that some agents will emphasize having a large number of listings. However, it doesn't necessarily mean those are really the best areas for you and your family. Speak to several agents before targeting one particular area.

Realty boards. A county board can be more objective than an individual agent and can point you toward areas where owners take pride in their homes, where houses sell quickly, and where property values remain high. In some areas, though, the boards are minimally staffed and you will be referred to member agencies rather than given information directly.

Homebuilders' associations. Check with the state or local association to find out which areas have seen the most dramatic growth in recent years. Where are the new developments? Which areas of town have the best-constructed older homes?

Remodeling contractors. Check with several local contractors to find out which neighborhoods are being improved and updated by residents. A well-kept area adds value to the homes there and, in turn, to the value of the entire area.

Landlord associations. Check with local landlord associations to find out which areas have higher-than-average ratios of owner-occupied housing versus rental housing. The most desirable neighborhood is one with the highest possible percentage of owner-occupied housing units.

Insurance agents. A local insurance agent who sells a good volume of homeowner's insurance can tell you which neighborhoods have increased in value on a regular basis because homeowners in those areas have updated their coverage more frequently than homeowners in other areas. In addition, insurance agents can provide you with information about insurance costs in different parts of town.

Bankers and lenders. Few professionals know the local real estate market as well as bankers and lenders. Of course, real estate agents deal with the market all the time, but they are looking for commissions. Bankers, in comparison, know the business but don't profit directly from the decision you make. They can tell you which neighborhoods are good based on low foreclosure and delinquency rates.

Planning department. The local planning department of a town, city, or county can tell you whether or not the area is in a floodplain and can give you the historical background of flooding, mudslides, road quality, and other important information you need to know. Perhaps more critically, the planning department can tell you what is going to happen in the future. Ask for a copy of the local zoning laws and the neighborhood plan. (You may have to pay a small fee for these documents.) *Read the neighborhood plan.* This document tells you not only what the local government allows in the area, but also what future plans it has.

Fire department. Compare the number of fires in the neighborhood in recent months and years with the average number in the whole area or in the state. A high incidence of fires in a neighborhood, especially if they are arson or suspicious fires, is a sure sign that the neighborhood is in trouble.

Police department. Ask for statistics on crime rates. Are violent crime and property crime on the rise, or are they holding steady or declining? How does the area compare with adjacent communities in terms of overall police protection?

Local newspapers. Check back issues at the library to get a sense of the social and community issues of greatest interest in the area. If major issues will affect property values, you should know about them before you start the buying process. Be sure you understand the ramifications of such reports. You should also be aware that real estate agents are not likely to bring to your attention any negative community problems that could scare you off. Do your own research.

The neighbors. Perhaps the most important source of information about a neighborhood is the neighborhood itself. Talk to the people who might become your future neighbors. Ring doorbells and ask questions. If the response is friendly and enthusiastic, that's a sign of an amiable, secure, outgoing neighborhood. However, if the people hesitate to answer your questions, are guarded and defensive, or refuse to talk to you, that's a bad sign. Ask about the climate, traffic, noise, quality of schools, transportation, and shops, looking for positive and encouraging responses.

• •

A Neighborhood Checklist

Any evaluation of a neighborhood should include the following:

Transportation. Access to commuter rail lines, buses, and highways should be convenient.

Traffic. Increasing traffic means growth in the area. Too much, and the quality of life will suffer. If there is heavy traffic close to the home you're thinking of buying, the noise and pollution levels could negatively affect your life.

Privacy. Ideally, homes should be located on streets where residents can enjoy peace and quiet in their homes and yards.

Parking. Besides adequate personal parking close to the home, you will want ample parking spaces for any guests. A lack of parking space for visitors can be a major inconvenience.

Shopping. Large shopping centers should be within reasonable driving distance, but far enough away so that traffic doesn't affect you directly. Some smaller regional shopping outlets, like a corner grocery store, are great conveniences.

Churches or synagogues. Be sure your neighborhood is not too far from your preferred house of worship.

Schools. The quality of public (and private) schools in the area is of paramount importance, especially if you have children. However, even if you don't have children, there is a historical correlation between excellent schools and low crime rates in an area. For those with children, the home should be close enough so getting to school is easy, but preferably far away enough so that noise and student traffic is not an immediate problem. Be sure the school district provides transportation for students if the distance to school is too far to walk.

Hazards. Check to make sure there are no potentially hazardous areas nearby, such as quarries, polluted streams, or toxic waste dumps. Also inquire about the possibility of radon contamination in the area.

Noise level. Check for noise during peak traffic hours and throughout most of the day. Any nearby industry, airports, train access, or other sources of noise can be highly disruptive, especially in the summer months. Even an animal habitat can be a source of disturbance if it is located too close to your home.

Police protection. Make sure police regularly patrol the neighborhood, respond promptly to calls, and, in general, protect the homeowners and the area adequately. Talk to other people living in the neighborhood to determine the level of police protection. Is there a neighborhood watch? Do the police provide preventive and educational programs in the schools?

Fire services. Find out the distance from the neighborhood to the closest fire station. What is the typical response time to calls? Ask about the number of fires in the neighborhood during the past year, and also how far apart hydrants are located. How far is the closest hydrant to the home you're considering buying?

Emergency medical services. Does the community provide emergency response teams? How far away are their stations located and are they connected to the fire department, or are they private companies? What is the cost, if any, of an emergency response?

Hospitals. Find out how far the closest hospitals are, and determine the quality of their emergency rooms and the scope of their services. Make sure your favored form of health insurance is accepted by the local hospital and physicians.

Town planning. The best neighborhoods are planned carefully in advance of development, with conveniently arranged streets sensitive to traffic patterns and well-placed shopping centers and recreational facilities. Buffer zones between commercial and residential areas should be provided to ensure a high quality of life.

Neighbors. You should feel comfortable with your neighbors. If you have children, there should be other children in the area of similar ages.

Cultural outlets. How accessible are museums, libraries, and concert halls? Are clubs and organizations active in the neighborhood, and do different groups offer a diversity of social and cultural outlets for your family?

Recreational outlets. Make a note of the number of parks, restaurants, theaters, and other recreational facilities in and close to the neighborhood.

Climate. If the area is oppressively hot or cold for part of the year, be sure you and your family can tolerate those extremes in temperature. Also be prepared to live with exceptionally high heating or cooling bills.

Crime levels. Is crime increasing or decreasing? Inquire about the volume of property crimes in the neighborhood and try to find any trends. Check with the local police or sheriff for this information.

Terrain. Are a large number of homes located on hills or directly below potential slide areas? The steeper the grade and the more developed the area surrounding it, the greater the potential for problems. Find out whether any flooding or slide problems have occurred in the recent past, and also ask whether the neighborhood is part of a federal floodplain.

Utilities. Taste the tap water and ask local water supply authorities for recent reports on the quality of the water supply. During heavy rains, are residents warned to boil water before drinking it? Are there current problems with storm drains, sewer systems, or water facilities? Is water available from private wells, and what state regulatory restrictions are placed on further well drilling? Also ask about other utilities. What is the cost of gas and electric service? How promptly does the telephone company respond to hookup or repair calls? Is cable television available, and at what cost? Is garbage picked up regularly, and what does that cost? Does the local refuse company offer a recycling program?

Neighborhood improvements. Is the local government improving its buildings, parks, and other facilities? If so, that is a positive sign that the area is being managed well enough that the tax base can support maintaining current standards.

Local property taxes. Levies on property are important because they reflect the makeup of a community's tax base and indicate the range of community services, including schools, police and fire service, utilities, municipal improvements, and overall level of government service. Of particular interest to prospective homeowners is the rate of property tax escalation, which is often set by law, and the allocation of property tax funds in the community to various uses, as well as the method of appraising property and frequency of tax increases.

Zoning. Zoning rules should be strictly enforced. Make sure residential areas are free of commercial and industrial development. The county or city planning department can provide zoning maps and neighborhood plans. With that information in hand, check the neighborhood to see whether the statements in the plan and on the zoning map are being followed according to the rules.

● ●

6

How to Evaluate Homes

If you're like the average home buyer, your head will begin to swim after you've looked at a number of homes. In fact, you should look at as many homes as possible so that you will have a thorough basis for comparison as well as an understanding of what you can afford. Looking at a range of available homes helps you establish realistic expectations.

To evaluate a home, you should conduct a systematic search of comparable homes, use a checklist, and sketch the floor plan of every home you view. This will help you later, when the details and features of several homes become a blur and you try to sort it all out. If you look at three or more homes in the same afternoon, you may confuse features.

■ Explaining Your Preferences to the Agent

You'll probably look at homes in the company of a real estate agent. Either you will stop in at an open house being hosted by the agent, or you will meet the agent at the brokerage office and go from there to homes you'll view by appointment.

At an open house, an agent will show the home. If you stop by to see it, you are under no obligation to do business with that agent. However, attending open houses might be a good way to view homes while also looking for an agent. If you start out at the agent's office, though, be sure you and the agent have a complete understanding of what you're looking for—before you leave the office. This will save everyone a lot of time and trouble. Discuss the following preferences to the agent.

Location. By narrowing down the area, you also narrow down the number of homes you need to view. Going through dozens of homes is an exhausting and often discouraging process, especially if you aren't familiar with the neighborhood or don't think you can afford any of the homes you're seeing. Apply the criteria listed in Chapter 5 before setting foot in a single home. It will make your search much easier and will also enable the agent to better help you to find what you need and want.

Home style. If you understand the difference between styles like Cape Cod and Carpenter Gothic, you're a step ahead of the game. However, you don't need to be an architectural historian to be able to communicate with an agent about the type of home you're interested in viewing. If you have a very specific style in mind, find a picture in a magazine, cut it out, and give it to the agent.

Emphasize that you want to steer clear of any homes with poor design features, such as an odd exterior appearance and proportions, or a poorly constructed house with substandard building materials.

Size. Most home buyers will describe the home they want in terms of the number of bedrooms it should have, but there is more to consider.

First, try to anticipate your needs for the next 5 to 10 years. Assume either that you will be able to move up to a larger home if your family grows, or that you will prefer to add improvements later on. You might, for example, tell the agent that you need a house that you can add another bedroom to without trouble, or one with space that can be remodeled into an extra bedroom at a later date.

Also, be specific about the size of the living room, kitchen, and bathrooms you prefer. For some people, a garage is an essential feature, whether used for parking or storage, or just for future conversion;

for others, it is not very important if a house doesn't have a garage at all. Perhaps the size of bedrooms is critically important to you. If you are used to exceptionally large rooms, you might not be happy with the smaller bedrooms found in many newly built homes, especially those on the lower end of the pricing scale.

If you have looked at many homes and have paid attention to total usable space, you can be specific to the point of telling your agent how much square footage as well as the number of bedrooms and other features you need.

Price. This is, of course, the most commonly used (and most practical) guideline. It should not, however, be the only preference you express to the agent. If it is, you will be taking a hit-or-miss approach to buying a home. An agent cannot be expected to satisfy your requirements unless you thoroughly communicate your needs concerning area, size, style, and other features.

Be realistic. You are not going to find a mansion at fixer-upper prices, and if you are looking for your first home with a minimum down payment, a good portion of the market is going to be out of reach. When making your list of preferred features, you should also understand that price will limit your choices.

If you begin your search by reading ads in the local paper or real estate circular, prices are usually featured. (They elicit the most responses.) If you want a home in a particular community where the majority of homes there are above your price range, you may be interested in the lowest-priced one. After viewing several such low-priced homes, however, you may discover that:

- They are generally the most run-down homes on the market.
- They are in the poorer areas of town.
- There are likely to have problems such as chronic flooding or be in an inconvenient location.
- The floor plan is poor or the home does not conform well to other homes in the neighborhood.
- A lot of maintenance or renovation is required, meaning you will have to spend money just to bring it up to par.
- The homes are not as described.

Ads often have "come-ons" to attract you. Chances are that after a while, you will recognize the phrases and what they really mean. For example:

What the Ad Says	What It Really Means
Bring your hammer	The house is run-down
Cute cottage	Small
Rustic	Inconveniently located
Needs tender loving care	Has not been kept up
Owner financing	Turned down by the bank
Exceptional bargain	Structural problems

Take greater control of the home-buying process and become an informed consumer. Start out by giving the agent a list of your preferences, including:

- The area of town that you want to see.
- The precise house style (age, design, even a general floor plan) that you want.
- Size, including the size of the lot and sizes of the rooms.
- Price.

If you are told there's nothing on the market meeting all of your specifications, check with another agent before you decide whether or not to compromise your list. By the time you see an agent, you should already be aware of the market at least in general terms. The more informed you are at the beginning of the process, the better your chances of finding what you want.

■ Using Diagrams

Diagram the rooms of any home you are seriously considering buying. A rough sketch will suffice. It doesn't have to be something an interior decorator would be proud of, just a reminder for your own use. Be sure to include any special features such as split levels, fireplaces, or walk-in closets.

Use grid paper to create this diagram, estimating the size of each room and trying to keep the sketch as accurate as possible. Real estate

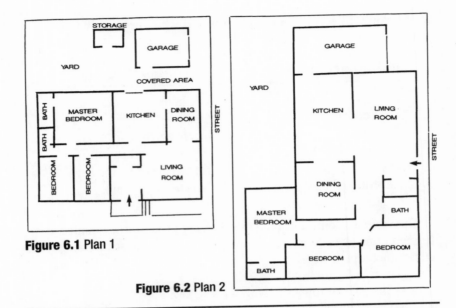

Figure 6.1 Plan 1

Figure 6.2 Plan 2

agents should be able to supply you with actual measurements of the rooms (listings are not always that complete).

Note the two diagrams above. The features of one house make it more acceptable than the other.

Good features (Plan 1):

- Privacy: those people inside the house are not within the view of the front entrance.
- Good use of space overall.
- As few corners as possible.
- Good overall shape and flow between rooms.
- Bathrooms are close together so that plumbing work is coordinated in the same part of the house.

Poor features (Plan 2):

- No privacy: people in the kitchen, dining room, or living room are in full view of the front entrance.
- Much wasted space.
- Garbled floor plan with too many corners.
- Odd overall shape for living space.

- Bathrooms are in different parts of the house, meaning more piping running underneath the floors and more expense in construction.

On your diagram, you can also jot down your immediate impressions of the home as you walk through it. You will spend 20 minutes or less in the typical home, more if you are impressed.

In homes you consider top prospects, take more time with your diagram, noting carefully the locations of all windows, doors, and closets. Make notes about the types of flooring, quality and condition of walls, doors, closets, and ceilings. Ask which appliances will be included and write down what you are told. Also jot down your comments about the exterior of a house: Comment on the landscaping, degree of maintenance the yard will need, appearance of the roof, how recently a house appears to have been painted, size of the lot, and your overall impressions of the property.

■ What Sells a Home

Conventional features help sell a home because a majority of buyers want these features and put them at the top of their wish lists. These include:

House appearance and style. Does the home conform with the size, shape, style, and period of the other homes on the block? Individuality is one thing; distinct nonconformity is another. In general, to safeguard your investment, a home should grow in value on a par with similar homes in the neighborhood, and to achieve a reasonable resale value, the home should be a good fit for the neighborhood, area, and climate.

Construction materials. Wood siding is still the most popular exterior material, although in warmer climates it is also the most susceptible to termite and beetle damage. Brick, stone, and granite are less common but highly desirable in warmer climates, whereas stucco is an attractive and generally acceptable building material, although it is subject to cracking in very cold weather. Aluminum and vinyl siding are practical and relatively maintenance-free, and are growing in popularity in some areas of new construction.

Landscaping, views, and siting. There is no doubt that a view substantially increases a home's value. The prospect of being able to take a daily glance at rivers or lakes, hills and mountains, wooded areas, or expanses of empty space is a tempting feature to any homeowner. For some, even the skyline of a big city is an exciting feature worth paying more for. But how absolutely necessary is that view and, more to the point, how much is it worth in the price of the home? That's your decision, of course. Be aware, however, that while the view might eventually pall, you will keep on paying for it for a long time to come.

An expanse of lawn is another feature to consider. A large piece of property, especially if it includes beautifully manicured lawns and shrubs, needs constant maintenance (except perhaps during the dead of winter). To maintain property value, you'll have to invest in upkeep, meaning your own time or a monthly expense to have someone else do it for you. If you enjoy gardening, that's fine. If you don't like the idea of a constant chore, choose a house with minimum lawn upkeep, perhaps with self-maintaining plantings and trees.

The actual siting or placement of a home becomes an important comfort feature once you have lived in it year-round. How many rooms face south and get the rays of the late morning or early afternoon sun? Do many rooms face north, having little or no direct sunlight? Is there too much shade from overhanging tree branches or shrubbery? These considerations will affect your heating and electric bills, not to mention resale value of the home.

You also have to think about privacy. Some screening trees or plantings will make a big difference. If you believe the house and yard are set up so that you have inadequate privacy from the street and from neighbors, yet the house is otherwise desirable, consider erecting an attractive fence or planting fast-growing shrubbery to achieve a screening effect.

Garages. Most buyers expect to get a garage with their house, even though many end up using it for purposes other than housing a car. Plenty of storage is a desirable feature. But this convenience is not always available, especially in older houses built before garages were popular. You might have to settle for a one-car garage when you really want a two-car type, and use a shed in the back yard to store other items like bicycles, yard tools, and equipment. Houses located above garages are unpopular because of the danger of automobile fumes. Detached garages are not as desirable as the attached variety, especially in colder regions, whereas carports are even more undesirable but have been accepted only in the warmer climates of the Southeast and Southwest.

Driveways. A steep incline will affect resale value because people don't want to risk damaging their car parking on the property or getting to the garage. This is especially true in colder climates, where garages are essential because snow and ice create drainage problems and driving hazards. In general, a blacktop or concrete driveway is the most desirable type. Gravel driveways tend to become muddy in wet weather, dusty in the summer heat, and generally messy year-round.

Terraces, decks, porches, and patios. Most homeowners are attracted to outdoor areas for warm-weather relaxing, outdoor games, or barbecues. Flagstone or concrete patios or terraces add charm and atmosphere for outdoor relaxation. Decks and porches, depending on the style of the home, are among the most desirable outside features. Roofed and screened porches are especially convenient in extreme weather climates.

Windows. In colder climates, combination storm and screen windows are appreciated additions to any home. Self-insulating, double-paned windows are found in virtually all new homes and have become standard.

Entrances. First impressions are always important. An attractive front entranceway and an adequate foyer can increase a home's market appeal tremendously. However, the back door probably will get as much use as the front, so a mud room, enclosed porch, or hallway for storing boots and coats is a great convenience. If a laundry room is also close to the back, it is well situated.

Traffic patterns. A convenient flow of traffic in a home is important to the routine of daily living. Survey your prospective home and ask yourself: How many rooms have to be walked through to get from one point to another? Are bedrooms sufficiently separated from the living room and kitchen areas? Is the family room close to the kitchen? Can you get to the kitchen by more than one route? Is the bathroom conveniently located for guests? All of these points will affect your lifestyle and comfort in the years to come.

Kitchens. The kitchen is certainly the most utilized room for most families. It is also among the most important features for resale value.

A kitchen with room for an eating area and with plenty of counter room and cabinets is the most sought after by most home buyers. Modern, up-to-date appliances are adjuncts of a practical, desirable kitchen, along with a supply of natural light, adequate storage space for brooms and cleaning materials, and, if possible, a laundry room close by. A pantry is a definite plus. Remember that kitchen expansions (remodeling jobs) are expensive, and a generously sized, well-planned kitchen is a plus.

Bathrooms. As with kitchens, modern, up-to-date bathrooms are prime considerations for most home buyers. A master bathroom plus a second bathroom in the hall increases the value of a home by at least the amount it takes to build that second bath. A bathroom located close to the living room or family room is even more desirable, especially for families with children or families that entertain a lot. In two-story homes, having a bathroom on both floors is practically a necessity. Check tiles in bathrooms for cracking or loose grout, signs that tile work will be required in the near future. Also, check water pressure in bathrooms. Do the rooms include a bath-shower combination? Is ventilation adequate? Is there a window or a fan, and what is your preference? For second-floor bathrooms, is there any sign of water damage on the ceiling in the room below?

Living room. A large living room is a popular feature in a home, especially when there is no family room. Ideally, the living room should be apart from the noisier areas of the home, usually a family area where children play or watch television. Living rooms should provide quieter areas where adults can talk or read. A fireplace is a bonus, even when it isn't used very often. Some people won't buy a house if it doesn't have a fireplace in the living room. If you buy a house with this feature, be sure to have the flue and chimney checked out before the deal is closed; and if the fireplace hasn't been used for several months, it should be inspected before use.

Dining room. A formal dining room is desirable for most buyers, especially those who want to entertain. However, a dining area off the kitchen is adequate for most people, since most homes do not offer a separate room. The dining room or area should be right off the kitchen, with access through a door or around a short corner.

Family room. Home buyers, especially those with children, appreciate family rooms on the first floor. This takes a lot of pressure off the living room, and this room can also serve as an entertainment center for the entire family. For adults, being able to separate the children in their own area provides peace and quiet. Basement family rooms are out of favor and no longer desirable; however, if well designed and insulated, a basement room can still serve as an acceptable alternative, especially in smaller homes with limited floor plans and space.

Laundry room. A separate laundry room on the first floor is a real luxury and increases resale value. In modern construction, the laundry room is often found in a short hallway area between the garage entrance and kitchen. As a secondary arrangement, a washer and dryer located in or near the kitchen is acceptable, often enclosed in a closet with an accordion door or sliding door so the appliances are not always visible. Basement laundry areas are less popular but common. That requires more travel within the house to wash and dry clothes and then to transport them back to bedrooms. Some designers actually place laundry rooms near bedrooms, on the theory that less travel distance to clothing storage areas makes sense. It adds desirability to locate storage shelves and hanging areas close to the washer and dryer, space permitting.

Closets. Is it possible to have too much closet space? A walk-in closet in the master bedroom is attractive to just about every buyer. Linen closets, foyer coat closets, broom closets, and a storage closet close to the back door are all practical features.

Attics. The big, old-fashioned attic used for storage of family treasures is found only in older, bigger houses. It's desirable to have a lot of storage space within the house, but attics are inconvenient. It is difficult to transport heavier goods up to an attic, often because the last leg up is a very steep stairway. Pull-down stairs are acceptable and space-saving, but closet or garage storage is far more convenient.

Basements. Home buyers expect adequate-size, dry basements, if only for utility and storage. Good lighting and access to the outside are also desirable features. Newer houses, notably in warmer climates, often offer utility rooms somewhere off the garage as an alternative to the more historical basement area. The basement, containing the foundation as well as heating, electrical, and plumbing systems, is the core of the house. A serious home buyer should thoroughly inspect the basement with a flashlight and hire a professional inspector to check all systems. The basement is easier to check than the crawl spaces in more modern construction. Some items to check for in the basement include:

- Termite damage: It's difficult to determine if a house is adequately protected against the ravages of termites. Rather, look for signs of termite damage: telltale mud tunnels or evidence of recent swarmings. Tunnels are the transportation system for subterranean termites, used to travel between the earth and the wood of the house. Termites cannot expose themselves to the open air for any period of time, so they depend on the tunnels and tubes to get around. During swarming, or the mating flight of termites, they shed their wings. Hundreds of dried wings found on sills and floor areas are definite signs of a full-scale termite invasion. We strongly recommend that you hire a pest inspection service to perform a thorough inspection of any property on which you have made an offer. The inspection should be a condition of your offer. (See Chapter 8 for other conditions.)
- Signs of water damage: Look for water stains along the bottom of the basement walls. If it is apparent that there has been water damage in the past, find out why and when, or hire a professional contractor to examine the entire basement area. Some water problems can be solved, others cannot. In some instances, a sump pump can help. You might notice a white fuzz on the walls of the basement or garage. This is called *efflorescence* and is caused by moisture and acids in the concrete. A little efflorescence is not serious, but a large amount calls for more investigation, since it points to chronic moisture and dampness.
- Settling: Every new house settles a bit over time, and you will probably find hairline cracks in most basement foundation walls. But large foundation cracks indicate uneven settling and merit further inspection by a professional. Another sign of suspicious settling is doors or windows that bind or show signs of cracking.

• •

A Basic Checklist

As a prospective homeowner, arm yourself with a flashlight and checklist. When viewing a home, pay attention to:

Walls and ceilings. Check for cracks and holes, especially in plaster walls and ceilings. Seams in wallboard should be invisible and smooth. Be alert for any signs of water damage, such as staining or peeling.

Floors. Hardwood floors are highly valued but need periodic care. What is the condition of flooring underneath carpeting? If you can take a look underneath, fine. But if it's wall-to-wall carpeting, you'll probably have to take the current owner's word that the floors are in good condition. Even without seeing floors, however, you can often tell whether or not they're in good repair. Floors that move when you walk on them, that feel uneven, or that make noise when you pass over them may be in disrepair.

Attic. If it's accessible, check for water leaks and any signs of rodent infestation. Leaks will show as dark stains on the wood of rafters, especially around chimney and ventilation areas. Droppings and shredded nesting materials in corners are sure signs of infestation by squirrels, bats, or mice. Make sure there is adequate ventilation, with vents in roofs allowing excess heat and moisture to escape. Check the amount and type of insulation between roof rafters and floor joists in the attic area.

Roof. The most common roofing material used in this country is asphalt shingles, which normally last between 15 and 20 years. If you observe bare spots on shingles or they are badly worn or curling, the house will need a new roof in the next few years. Be sure you have the roof included in a thorough inspection. Check gutters and downspouts as well. These are usually made of aluminum or plastic and are relatively maintenance-free. Some older homes will have wooden gutters, which should be thoroughly inspected for signs of rotting or leaking.

Electrical system. You'll need a professional inspector or electrician to thoroughly review the electrical system, especially in an older home, but you can spot some danger signs yourself. Does the house include 220-volt wiring adequate to run air conditioners, electric ranges, dryers, and other appliances? Check the circuit breaker or the main electrical board to determine whether it carries 220. If an older house still runs on fuses, it would be better to upgrade to a circuit breaker system. Also, ensure that there are enough outlets in each room, at least one for every 10 to 12 feet of wall space, and that all outlets and switches are properly covered. Exposed wiring or wires that hang without being enclosed and capped are a potential hazard and might also indicate other problems you cannot see.

Heating system. Gas and oil furnaces are the most common type of heating systems found in American homes. Your chief concern should be the overall efficiency of the system in the house you're looking at. What does it cost to heat the house in the coldest months of the year? Ask whether you can have a summary of the homeowner's heating bills for the last 12 months to get a complete picture of the heating system's cost. An inspector can also check the unit's efficiency and recommend a regular maintenance schedule. Added insulation can also help to minimize the need for using the system during months that are not so cold. Also, check the thermostat. Does it work efficiently? Does it include an automatic setting? Are there thermostats in each room?

Hot water heater. This should be thoroughly checked out by a qualified inspector. Ask whether the hot water heater is a circulating system attached to the furnace (it has no storage capacity, and the furnace must stay on even in the summer, if only to heat water) or a freestanding hot water system (an 80-gallon tank will ensure sufficient hot water for a family of four). An electrical unit is more expensive to run than a gas unit. Check the age of the water heater. If it is older than 12 years, it may have to be replaced in the near future.

Plumbing. You will have difficulty judging the condition of the plumbing on sight. Unless the house is recently constructed, about the only thing you can ascertain is whether the pipes are brass, copper, galvanized iron, or polyvinyl chloride (PVC) plastic. Look for obvious signs of leaking, low water pressure, or noise when plumbing is in use. Beyond these obvious signs, rely on a professional inspector to evaluate the condition of the plumbing system.

Water supply and waste disposal. If you are considering buying a house with its own well water, be sure you have the water tested beforehand. Check the supply—is it adequate throughout the year? If the house has a cesspool or septic system for disposal, have the entire system inspected by a qualified professional. How often does the tank have to be drained, and when was the last time that maintenance was performed? Make sure you know the exact location of the tank, and get the name and telephone number of the company that provides maintenance for the system.

7

Making an Offer

A seller places a house, condominium, or co-op on the market hoping to attract serious buyers. The asking price is usually a guideline—a general indication of what would be acceptable to the seller.

We refer to the price as a guideline because offers can be made below or, in some situations, above that price. For example, two buyers who want the same house may bid against each other, exceeding the asking price. The price the seller announces is a starting point.

When a buyer makes an offer and the seller accepts, a contract is created. In order for a real estate contract to be valid and enforceable, it has to contain the following four elements:

1. It must be in writing. Verbal contracts are not binding in real estate transactions. In law, verbal contracts are usually valid, but real estate transactions are exempted from that general guideline. Even for other arrangements, verbal agreements are troublesome; in the event of a problem, both sides may disagree as to what the terms were unless they are put in writing. There's an old expression worth remembering: A verbal contract isn't worth the paper it's written on.

2. The contract must include an offer and acceptance statement. This

establishes mutual consent between the two sides. In real estate, the buyer and the seller must consent before a contract can exist.

3. The contract has to be legal. If a contract violates the law, it is invalid. For example, under the law both sides have to be of age and mentally competent. Without these requirements, there can be no contract. Or, if a contract contains a provision that is itself illegal, it cannot be enforced under the law.

4. The contract has to include consideration, meaning that something of value has to be given by one side in exchange for something of value. There is no contract if only one side is required to comply. For example, the buyer pays an agreed-upon price for a home, for which the seller agrees to surrender title. When both sides act upon their contractual obligations, they are said to have performed. Examples of performance include paying closing costs and a down payment, getting financing approved, completing repairs or inspections, and signing the closing documents that transfer title.

If at any time during negotiations for a house, condo, or co-op, you are not sure whether you are committing yourself to a contract, *find out before you sign anything*. Without careful and thorough examination of what you're signing, you might end up under contract when you thought you were only testing the waters. If, even after checking every aspect of a deal, you are unsure about the degree of commitment you are making, ask more questions and, if necessary, speak to your attorney.

In the case of condominiums, the review of legal documents is even more complex. You need to understand all of the terms in the *Declaration of Condominium,* and should also read the bylaws of the association.

If you are thinking of buying a co-operative apartment, carefully check the offering plan and ask your attorney to review it as well. Also, read the bylaws, the latest financial statement of the corporation, and the proprietary lease.

When purchasing any property, the contract is rarely entered into on the first round of discussions. In negotiating the deal, there often will be numerous offers and counteroffers between buyer and seller before the actual price and other terms are agreed upon. Your best offer, even when not initially accepted by the seller, may be accompanied by an "earnest-money" check or commitment note to demonstrate your good faith in going through with the deal. Without such a commitment, a buyer might make numerous offers without following through on them, which would complicate the real estate transaction and make it impossible to seriously negotiate. All offers and counteroffers must be in writing, including even minor changes in terms.

If your offer is accepted, a contract is drawn up between buyer and seller, and conditions and contingencies are specified as part of the contract. Contingencies are requirements that have to be met as part of the deal in order to make the contract binding. For example, a standard contingency is that the buyer has to obtain financing approval by a specified deadline. Another contingency is that the seller has to complete certain inspections to the buyer's satisfaction, including supplying an inspection report.

Every contract should provide for three critical contingencies. Financing is the first contingency and is part of virtually every contract, except those rare contracts in which the buyer pays all cash or the seller is willing to finance the whole deal. The second contingency is the pest inspection. The third contingency is the contractor or structural inspection. For older homes, more specialized inspections (plumbing, electrical, and heating systems) should also be included as contingencies.

As the contract proceeds, some amendments might be offered. For example, you might negotiate with the seller for appliances or furniture to be included in the deal. Or when an inspection report is issued, some work might be required, so you may want to amend the deal to specify a deadline and who will pay for the work. Such matters can be executed by way of written amendments to the contract.

■ The Competition

Some home buyers may find the perfect house, condo, or co-op, only to be inched out of the deal by another buyer with a slightly better offer. If you desperately want a particular property, you can do any of the following:

- Make an offer at or close to the asking price. This will demonstrate that you are seriously interested.
- Do not attach any contingencies to your offer. Contingencies may include selling a previous house, obtaining financing, in-

spections and repairs the seller is expected to perform, and deadlines for vacating the house.

Note: Bypassing contingencies can be very risky, and you might want to get some legal advice first.

- Offer a higher-than-average deposit to demonstrate that you are a serious buyer. You don't have to limit your offer to what the real estate agent indicates is the minimum deposit, which is common practice. Depending upon how interested you are, your deposit can exceed the minimum.
- Offer to pay the seller's closing costs or the cost of inspections.

Remember, however, that if you do any of these things, you will also lose negotiating leverage. If you demonstrate such a high degree of desire that you give the seller too much of an advantage, you could pay dearly for your eagerness. There is a risk that the seller will make a counteroffer that includes more demands than you're willing to concede.

Successful negotiation—offer, counteroffer, and acceptance—involves maintaining a delicate balance. Ideally, you want to express your sincerity without giving up everything before the discussions have begun. This is why having an agent can be so valuable. The agent should not only know how to make a deal, he or she should be detached enough to represent both sides and to offer reasonable compromises that may lead to a satisfactory and fair contract.

■ Buyer's and Seller's Markets

Competition for a particular property depends on its desirability. It may be a home of historic importance or it may be a particularly exceptional bargain with an ideal location in a desirable neighborhood. The more desirable the property, the more buyers will be attracted to it. These and other factors of the supply and demand cycle will determine whether you will find yourself in a buyer's market or a seller's market.

Try to buy—and later sell—when perfect market conditions exist. For the buyer, you want a lot of competitively priced homes to be available at the same time. Later, when you become a seller, you will want a large number of anxious buyers bidding against one another to win your property. Many homeowners have been fortunate to have experienced both ideal conditions. Others have not been so lucky. Because market conditions are beyond your control, you might find yourself buying in a seller's market or, later, trying to sell in a buyer's market.

As mentioned, making an offer in either market should begin with the complete neighborhood and home inspections. An informed buyer who thoroughly knows the market, the area, and the qualities and attributes of a home will always do better than one who is uninformed.

Even in a buyer's market, there are potential pitfalls and opportunities. The opportunities occur when there are more sellers than buyers (allowing you to take your time and evaluate several properties, selecting the best possible home for your money). Or when lenders are eager for business and, thus, are more likely to offer you a competitive rate and terms, not to mention prompter service and response.

Make sure, however, that you understand *why* it's a buyer's market, and how the economic factors will affect the future market value of your home. For example, your home may have hidden flaws common to all of the houses built in an area or by a particular builder or developer. The area might be subject to annual flooding, or crime might be on the rise as the neighborhood declines. An all-too-common problem occurs when a large employer lays off a large segment of its work force all at once. Pay particular attention if *you* will be working for that employer. However, if you are immune from employment risks—either because you are self-employed or because of your occupation—then you may find a good bargain without also being exposed to the risks.

In a buyer's market, with so many homes to choose from, you might be less apt to do all of the necessary preliminary investigations and inspections. You might reason that in such a market, you can dictate terms to eager sellers and lenders, so why bother? If you decide that research is not important because bargains are plentiful, you're only asking for trouble. No real estate investment is risk-free, and you should always know (to the best of your ability) what you're getting into.

Research in any kind of market is essential. Informed buyers reduce their risks because they arm themselves with the facts. Just because a market favors your position does not mean that all of the risks have been eliminated. In fact, even under favorable conditions, there is risk because of a buyer's tendency to relax and be less vigilant.

In a seller's market, the rules are the same but the approach is different. In such a market, the pressure is on the buyer. Sellers dictate the terms of sale. Even problem homes can be sold in a seller's market, and might be pushed the hardest. Make an offer with the competition in mind and with an eye on the economic conditions ruling the market. But follow the rules of common sense, and don't buy without first gathering all of the facts.

In a seller's market, don't allow yourself to be rushed into a decision you're not sure of, even if it means passing up what might be a bargain. Be thorough in looking for mortgage financing. Since lenders in the area will probably be demanding higher rates than you would find in a buyer's market, you need to shop around for the best possible terms.

Be sure you understand *why* it is a seller's market. Are current factors likely to change in the near future? If so, would it be wise for you to wait until they do? What are the likely risks of waiting? Don't allow preoccupation with the competition to cut short the necessary investigations of the area and of the home itself. If you do your preliminary homework, you'll be way ahead of the competition and be better able to spot a real bargain when it comes along.

■ Contingency Offers

Even if you are familiar with the area, the home, and the supply and demand market factors that are at work, your offer may not necessarily be enough. There may be a need for several contingencies attached to your offer.

As stated, a contingency is a qualification or condition added to the contract. In other words, a promise is made to abide by the contract only *if* the seller takes a specified action or upon the buyer's completion of a specified action—usually within a deadline.

A contingency that requires the seller to perform certain tasks is common in real estate transactions. The seller is often required to make needed repairs or pay for pest control work, for example. Or the buyer might make an offer contingent upon the results of a professional structural inspection, leaving open the possibility of further negotiations about paying for the cost of repairs. If that inspection turns up a problem, you then have the option of expanding the contingency by asking the seller to do the work by a set deadline; at that time, the seller might want to negotiate with you to split the cost or ask you to pay for the work.

Contingencies beyond the seller's control are more problematic for both sides. For both buyers and sellers, one of the most difficult contingencies to deal with is the precondition that a previous home has to be sold. "Contingent upon the sale of an existing home" means that when you make an offer, you can't close until you complete the sale of the home you're currently living in. Many otherwise perfect deals have collapsed because another home didn't sell quickly enough. Depending on the market, a real estate agent might discourage this contingency. Sellers might also impose a time limit for the contingency. Upon expiration of the allotted time, you have to either remove the contingency and buy the home anyway, or the deal is off.

Another common contingency, one that is standard in most contracts, is that the buyer obtain financing approval. This also comes with a deadline. If you cannot get approval for a loan, for whatever reason, the deal will collapse and the seller will look for another buyer.

In highly competitive markets, sellers often entertain offers from more than one buyer. If the first offer expires or a contingency is not met, the backup offer is accepted. In that case, the seller is assured of a second chance to complete the sale. The first buyer, meanwhile, has to start all over again.

■ The Offer

There are no standard formulas for making offers that are likely to be accepted. Every buyer and every seller is different, and we all have our own priorities and individual preferences. In addition, the state of the local real estate market, the desirability and condition of the property, and how badly you really want it will all affect your offer and the seller's response. It's wise, though, to ask some questions about the sales profile of the home you have in mind before making an offer, such as:

- How long has the house been on the market?
- Has the price been reduced since it was listed?
- Have previous offers been made?
- Did those offers fall through, and why?
- How does the asking price compare with the asking price of other homes?
- Is the asking price flexible or firm?

All of these questions may affect your approach and strategies in the offer-making process. (The agent might hesitate to answer some questions, especially if previous offers have fallen through.) Previous offers should remain confidential, in all fairness to the seller. However, if an offer fell through because the buyer-to-be had a financing problem, it would explain why a home has been on the market for several months and has not been sold.

Negotiating an offer is a delicate process. The buyer and seller have to compromise in order to reach an agreement. If one side is too inflexible or asks for too much, there will be no deal. A neutral and objective intermediary, usually an agent (or agents for each side), presents offers and counteroffers and conducts the negotiations. Buyers and sellers rarely meet during this phase, if ever. The agent handles all discussions and conveys information between the sides. It is critical to remember that every detail of the final offer *must* be put down in writing. It is too easy to leave out a few details, then end up fighting in court because a late modification was never clearly spelled out or signed off on.

Many buyers automatically assume that any offer within 10 percent of the asking price will be seriously considered. However, if the seller has several offers to review, you could miss an opportunity. A seller can always counter your initial offer, requiring a response from you. Negotiations bog down when both sides become unwilling to give any more ground. Surprisingly, this might occur at a point when the buyer and seller are only a few hundred dollars apart. That's where a smart real estate agent should intervene and point out to one or both sides that with a little more flexibility, everyone can get what they want.

You have considerably more leverage when the market is "soft." If a seller needs to sell quickly, or if the home has defects making it less marketable than most other homes, the price should reflect those conditions, and you should alter your bidding strategies based on those conditions.

In any case, all offers and counteroffers should be made in a timely manner. One to three days is standard unless the other person lives so far away that communication is difficult. Procedures for all of these matters vary; therefore, you should follow the advice of a real estate agent you trust. Your attorney can make the offer in your behalf. Attorneys or escrow officers are also helpful once the contract has been entered.

8

Outside Services

What happens if you make an offer on a home, hand over a large down payment, and go to the closing only to discover later that the property has a serious defect? If you're like most people who have just bought a home, your budget may be too severely strained to cover the cost of repairs. Fortunately, you can take steps *before you buy* to prevent this type of disaster from happening. Some of these safeguards are required by law or by lenders before any financing will be approved. In some parts of the country, for example, inspections for pests, especially termites, are mandated by law. However, even when not mandatory, you should take all necessary steps to ensure that hidden defects are revealed before the deal is closed. For example, if a home is situated on a steep slope and you're concerned about the danger of sliding or erosion, ask for a soil test from an engineer who specializes in that field. For a fee of a few hundred dollars, you can find out whether there is a potentially dangerous situation.

As to the cost of inspections, you should negotiate those with the seller. As a general rule, pest inspections are paid for by the seller; any additional inspections may be paid for by either side, depending on the circumstances and on who wants the inspection. For example, if your lender demands an electrical inspection as a condition of financing, you will probably be expected to pay for it.

■ Diagnostic Services

Inspections of the structure and systems are commonly performed before the sale of a home. It may be called a diagnostic-service inspection, a contractor's inspection, a home inspection, or a structural inspection. The trend has come about partly because of the increase in relevant court cases. Recently, the courts have been holding real estate agents and brokers liable for disclosure of defects. The courts have concluded that a broker or agent has a duty to find out whether or not there are any defects, and to tell potential buyers about them. The result has been the growth of the home-inspection business. To the buyer, an inspection is added insurance against the possibility that serious, hidden defects will have to be corrected later. This may be one of the most important contingencies in your contract. If any serious flaws are discovered, you may want to negotiate with the seller to either pay for repairs or lower the price of the home. In the future, the home-inspection contingency is likely to become a standard clause.

Few states require that home inspectors hold professional licenses. That means that in some areas anyone can set themselves up as a home inspector and offer to perform professional diagnostic services.

One national trade group, the American Society of Home Inspectors (ASHI), can help you find a qualified inspector. Individual ASHI members are not supposed to make repairs or refer you to a different contractor to perform the repairs. As a result, they can remain entirely objective. They are paid only to complete the inspection and provide a written report of their findings. However, because home inspectors are liable for nondisclosure of defects just as real estate agents are, they tend to be extremely thorough, if only to protect themselves in the event that you find a defect later. For information about how ASHI qualifies and tests its members, write to ASHI at 85 West Algonquin Road, Suite 360, Arlington Heights, IL 60005-4423, or call 800-743-2744 (or 708-290-1919).

If there are concerns regarding structural integrity, erosion, or adequacy of internal systems, ask for an engineering inspection. Contact the National Academy of Building Inspectors (NABI) for a referral to a qualified engineer in your area. Members must belong to the National Society of Professional Engineers and hold a current state license. NABI's address is 650 Brighton Avenue, Portland, ME 04102; telephone number, 207-828-1977.

The procedures for an inspection vary from one service to another, even among ASHI members. The degree of detail dictates the total cost, which may range between $175 and $350. However, every inspection should include a check of:

- Doors and windows
- Ceilings, walls, and floors
- Septic tanks and wells
- Insulation
- Plumbing and electrical systems
- Ventilation
- Roofing
- Foundations
- Heating and air-conditioning systems

The inspection does not necessarily cover compliance with local building codes, although many inspectors will check for compliance and will discuss it in their reports. The inspection report is not a guarantee or warranty.

The written report should be supplied as part of the service, but even so, it makes sense for you to be on hand when the inspection is conducted, especially if you are paying for the inspection. If the seller is paying for it, however, you will need to get permission to accompany the inspector. You can learn a lot about home maintenance and how to prevent future problems by asking the inspector questions.

Armed with such knowledge, you can negotiate for adjustments in the price or make an offer contingent upon the seller repairing a problem. Or you can ask for the seller to share in the cost of repairs.

In cases that have gone to court for nondisclosure, buyers have sued both the seller and the real estate agent. Such cases are extremely expensive and often take months or even years to resolve. Real estate agents in many areas insist on a home inspection as a matter of course just to protect themselves under the existing disclosure rules. The relatively minor cost of an inspection is a worthwhile investment, and could save you thousands of dollars and hours of time in the event of a dispute.

■ Getting a Home Warranty

Another form of protection is the home warranty. One of the most widely used programs in the United States is the Home Owner's Warranty (HOW) program, offered by builders of new homes. The warranty is included in the price of the home. HOW is currently available on approximately one-fourth of all new homes built.

The program covers any and all defects in workmanship and materials for the first year, as well as flaws in plumbing, electrical, heating, cooling, and mechanical systems. Warranty of workmanship is dropped after the first year, although major structural defects are covered for ten years. The warranty includes a deductible—you will have to pay the first $250 of repair costs during the first two years of the warranty if the builder fails to make repairs and a claim to HOW is made.

The new-home warranty is primarily a selling tool. For the builder and the program sellers, the chances of breakdown in brand new construction are relatively small. For the new homeowner, peace of mind is achieved. You should wonder, however, what real value you're getting from the warranty.

Also available through some national real estate firms and private companies is an older-home warranty. With the greater likelihood of systems breaking down in older homes than in newer ones, this warranty appears to make more sense. However, it costs between $245 and $400 *per year,* making it fairly expensive. Making matters worse, you will be charged between $35 and $100 for each service call, if needed. Considering the cost, it's doubtful that such warranties are ever justified. If you do get such a contract, carefully read the fine print. You will discover that the broad range of conditions and exceptions make most of these warranties risky.

Sellers are more likely to benefit from buying a warranty for one year as a condition of sale, to protect themselves in the event that defects come up that were not discovered through inspection. As a buyer, you should *not* skip a professional home inspection just because a warranty is provided for you or you buy one yourself.

Some home inspectors offer older home warranties as part of their inspection. The cost ranges between $200 and $500. For older homes and homes with a high likelihood of problems, such a warranty can be granted with specified exclusions. These warranties are often limited to three years, after which time you might be able to buy a renewal policy.

Whether or not you believe a warranty would be a sound investment, remember to compare the cost to the value. Read the exclusions of the warranty, and make sure you understand what is covered and what is not covered.

■ The Appraisal

The appraisal—a process to estimate the current market value of a home—is usually ordered by the bank or mortgage company considering your loan. You pay for the appraisal, and you are entitled to a copy of the report, but you will usually get one only if you ask. Some sellers order appraisals when they place their property on the market; however, your lender will probably expect you to pay for a new appraisal, even though a recent one is available.

The appraiser compares the home with similar homes in the area that were recently sold. Ideally, a similar home in a similar neighborhood will reveal the true market value of the home you're thinking of buying. The appraiser tries to find two or three comparable homes. When comparing similar homes with somewhat different features, the appraiser adjusts the estimate upward or downward. For example, a comparable home might have less square footage, a larger lot, or a better view. Or the house you're thinking of buying might have one additional bathroom, a more modern kitchen, or nicer landscaping.

The appraiser compares the home you're looking at to those comparable homes and comes up with an estimated value. The appraiser might also estimate the cost to replace or rebuild the home based on the current cost per square foot of building materials and labor. The two methods of estimation—market comparison and replacement cost—are then weighted or averaged, according to what the inspector believes to be fair. This is all detailed in the appraisal report.

In most cases, the lender uses an appraiser of their choice. However, if you will be ordering an appraisal, get referrals from one of two organizations: the Appraisers Association of America (212-889-5404) or the American Society of Appraisers (800-272-8258). Both require members to pass examinations and have at least five years of experience before they can be certified.

Watch out for any appraiser who charges a percentage of the appraised value. That is a clear conflict of interest. Most appraisal fees for houses range between $65 and $135 per hour, with minimums between $35 and $100. Some appraisers perform home appraisal reports for a set fee.

9

The Contract

The process of negotiating and finalizing a real estate contract is complex. If you work with a real estate agent, be sure he or she is willing to explain each and every part of the contract to you. Do not hesitate to ask questions. If you work with an attorney, be sure to hire one *before* you sign the contract. Preventing trouble is much easier than getting out of a bad situation you've committed yourself to on paper. Also, shop around. Not all attorneys charge the same rate, and you might be able to find excellent legal help at an affordable fee.

The contract process begins once you and the seller reach an agreement concerning price and other terms. The offer and counteroffer are made in contractual form, so you need to be aware of the terms during initial negotiations. A contract contains the names and addresses of buyer and seller, the address and legal description of the property being sold, the price and how it will be paid, and the closing date. Any contingencies are also spelled out in complete detail. Both sides sign the contract and date it. Following are the essential contingencies that should be included in every contract.

Home inspection. You should make sure that the property you are thinking of buying is in good condition. So many systems in a house, notably the expensive ones like plumbing, electrical, and heating, are out of sight and problems won't be apparent without an inspection. A home inspection should be ordered and completed as soon as possible after your offer has been accepted—in fact, in the contract itself, you may specify a deadline for completion of the inspection. Hire your own professional, one who is objective and qualified, and seek out a member of the American Society of Home Inspectors (ASHI) or a state association that applies similar standards. If repairs have to be made, you will probably be better off negotiating with the seller on the selling price and then hiring someone to do the work for you. By adjusting the price and getting your own contractor, you can be sure that the work is performed in a quality manner and that the problems are not just patched over.

Pest inspection. Termites are a greater problem in some parts of the country than in others. The farther south you live, the more of a threat this pest will be. A pest-control inspection should be undertaken automatically, even for newly constructed homes. There have been cases of termite-infested wood used in brand new homes, especially in the warmer southern states. By practice, the cost of the inspection is usually paid for by the seller. Repairs should be paid for by way of negotiation or absorbed by the seller. Some contingencies indicate a dollar amount the seller is willing to pay toward pest-control work. If required work exceeds that limit, you can void the contract, pay the difference, or negotiate again with the seller.

Mortgage financing. Unless you have enough cash to pay the entire purchase price, you will have a financing contingency in the contract. It is a standard clause because, with few exceptions, first-time buyers need to borrow most of the money to buy the home. Securing a mortgage loan can be an expensive, tedious, time-consuming process, but this contingency is the most vital part of your contract. The terms of the mortgage, percentage or amount of the purchase price, and time limit for securing a loan are all spelled out in the contract, and it's important to include all of these details. If, for any reason, your financing is not approved according to these terms, the contract is void. However, without this contingency, you would be likely to lose any money deposited for defaulting on your offer. The mortgage contingency normally includes a deadline. You must obtain approval by that date or you will lose all your rights under the deal and the contract will expire. As long as the deadline is reasonable, it can be used as leverage with a lender who is slow to grant approval of your loan application.

Title contingency. Another standard clause in most real estate contracts states that title must be "free and clear." That means that the owner does, in fact, have clear title and that title is not disputed or in doubt in any respect. All liens (loans and claims on the property) are to be disclosed and should be settled at closing. A title company conducts a title search, which is a record of all recorded notifications concerning the property. The buyer invariably buys a title insurance policy, which costs a one-time premium and remains in effect as long as you own the property. That insurance guarantees you that you will get clear title. If any liens are discovered later, your title insurance protects you. For example, if the seller borrowed $10,000 from a relative the day before closing and quietly recorded the note, and the title company did not discover that recording, it would be an undisclosed lien. However, since your title insurance ensures that you are not liable for such liens, you would not have to pay the $10,000. The title insurance company would have to pay off the lien for you as part of your coverage, and would then try to recover the money from the seller. Legal customs and laws regarding titles vary from one state to another. Check with your escrow agent, real estate agent, or attorney to find out how the laws work in your area.

You may have to deal with additional, less common contingencies in your contract, such as clauses that state which furniture, fixtures, or appliances will remain, and which will be taken by the seller; that the property be maintained by the seller until closing, including yard work, cleaning, and general repairs; or that you have the right to a final inspection before closing.

If you are selling your current home and buying another, you might want to add a contingency that the new deal is valid only if and when you sell your current home. If you include such a contingency, the seller will probably insist on a reasonable deadline, after which you either have to proceed with the deal or it is called off. This is often a deal-killer because sellers don't want to have to wait on a contingency they cannot control.

Escrow. One of the most confusing aspects of the contract process is escrow. This is the temporary holding of money (such as an earnest-money deposit) and documents. An escrow company or real estate attorney holds money and documents until all contingencies of the contract are satisfied.

The escrow agent also sets up a special trust fund—an escrow account—into which both buyer and seller deposit whatever funds are required by the terms of the transaction. For example, if a seller agrees to pay for an appraisal, a pest inspection, and certain repairs, the seller deposits the money in an escrow account. The buyer deposits an earnest-money check and, eventually, the balance of a down payment, as well as any other required funds. At the close of escrow, the escrow agent pays off all the lien holders, such as the seller's mortgage lender (as well as all inspectors), pays local recording fees and taxes involved in the transaction (as well as the real estate commission), and gives the seller the remaining proceeds. Then you and the seller sign the paperwork, and title is transferred. As a final step, the agent usually records the sale/purchase.

■ Things to Remember

The escrow process is designed to ensure that every step required by law is taken on your behalf. However, you should still make sure that all of the following occur before closing:

- All necessary inspections have been completed, and reports prepared and delivered. You should have reviewed the reports and made sure that you are satisfied that the related repairs have been made. Also, be sure that everyone agrees as to who is responsible for paying for repairs. If repairs have not been completed, make sure that arrangements are made to do the work and put it in writing, or make sure adjustments in proceeds have been made. Often, the timing of a contract's closing does not allow time to actually complete repair work. In such cases, the seller is asked to authorize a "hold-back," an amount of money kept in reserve pending completion of the work.
- The title company has determined that title is clear. The title report *and* title insurance policy should be issued and provisions made for a last-minute title search (common practice to ensure that no last-minute deeds or notes have been recorded).
- All mortgage contingencies have been met, and the lender is going to provide funds on your closing date according to terms agreeable to you.
- You have made arrangements for homeowner's insurance to cover the property, and the effective date is the same as the date

you will take title. If that date has been changed since you first arranged insurance, make sure you advise your insurance agent so the insurance date can be corrected.

- Make sure you and the seller have agreed upon the exact date the home will be vacated, and that all related conditions are agreed upon. These include delivery of all keys; arrangements for actual move-out and move-in times; which furniture, fixtures, and appliances will be left; and terms of payment for personal property not included in the real estate contract. When buyers move in before closing (which is rare) or when sellers remain in the home for a few days after closing (more common), you should have a rental agreement spelling out exact terms: daily rental amount, actual vacancy date, agreed-upon condition in which the property will be left, and a security deposit to be refunded only after you are satisfied that the home is in acceptable condition.

- Make sure you know the exact closing costs you will be expected to pay and the number of certified checks the escrow agent or attorney expects to have delivered at closing. Be sure you have enough cash on hand to pay for those checks the morning of closing or the day before. Minor adjustments can probably be settled by personal check. For example, if closing is moved up one day, that will change the accrued interest on your loan, and the proration of property taxes, utilities, and any other split expense between buyer and seller.

- Make sure you look at the property one last time to see that all work has been completed as stipulated in the contract. Remember, just because someone says work was completed doesn't necessarily mean it's true, or that it was done correctly. Resolve any differences before title is exchanged.

■ Holding Title

During the contract period, you will be asked how you want to hold title to your home. You have several choices, depending on the state where you live and where the home is located, including:

Joint tenancy. This is the most common and practical method of registration for a married couple; both people share the title to the home and the property is jointly owned. In the event of the death of one spouse, their half of the property's value is included in the estate. In most states it is possible to transfer property tax-free from one spouse to another, so that the surviving spouse ends up with a stepped-up basis—meaning that at the time of a homeowner's death, real estate is valued at the current market rate, which is usually higher than the original price for the property, and thus it is said to be stepped-up—for one-half of its value, which may become important later if the home is sold.

Tenancy in common. Under this arrangement, two people each own a portion of a house as "owners in severalty." There are two important considerations to this type of ownership. First, a single property owned in this manner is an undivided interest, meaning each owner cannot identify a portion of the property that they own apart from the other owners. Second, each tenant has the right to sell his or her interest without the consent of the other. For example, an unmarried couple may buy a home as tenants in common. A year later, one could sell his or her interest to someone else. (All states recognize this form of ownership, with special rules in effect in Louisiana.)

Ownership in severalty. You can own your home under one name only. This is legal in all states, and may be necessary if your spouse is a minor. Even though you register your home in this way, your spouse may be required to sign many of the documents required during escrow and to transfer title to the property. (All states recognize this form of ownership, with special rules in effect in Louisiana.)

The different forms of registration for ownership should be carefully considered before signing a contract and escrow documents, particularly by unmarried couples or people who want to share a home, or by residents of states that do not recognize joint tenancy. In those cases, you should seek legal advice. For married couples, joint tenancy makes a lot of sense because, upon the death of either spouse, there is no problem regarding valuation or transfer. Title simply passes to the surviving spouse.

10

Closing Costs

The purchase price you pay to the seller is not the only expense you agree to when you buy a home. As a first-time buyer, you need to be aware that you will face a baffling array of fees for everything from title insurance to property taxes. These fees are lumped together and are known as closing costs, since they are due and payable at the point of closing, as title passes from seller to buyer.

The closing process varies considerably from one part of the country to another. But the process and requirements of closing remain the same everywhere: At closing, all amounts due are paid, title is officially passed from seller to buyer, and the transaction is recorded at the local recorder's office. In response to numerous complaints by consumers about confusion at closing, Congress passed the Real Estate Settlement Procedures Act (RESPA) in 1974. Under RESPA, lenders are required to provide you with a list of closing costs as well as a list of the documents and services that must be presented or completed before closing. Because actual closing costs aren't known until around the closing date, RESPA requires that a best estimate of costs be given to you.

For tax purposes, you should know that some closing costs are deductible. Others are not, and have to be added to the cost of the home.

The final cost of buying a home, with additions of closing costs, is called the adjusted basis, which is the true total cost of your new home. This is important information. Later, when you sell your home, you need to compute the adjusted basis in order to report the taxable profit on the sale. Or, if you reinvest in another residence within two years, you need the information to compute the adjusted basis on the new home.

Following is a list of closing costs you will probably pay when you buy your home. These will vary by location and even by title, depending on customs in your area.

■ Lender Fees

Points. Also called loan discount fees or *loan fees,* a point is 1 percent of the amount you borrow. A lender may charge one or several points for granting you the mortgage loan. In markets where lenders are shopping for buyers—usually meaning rates are high but money is available for loans—points are minimal. Lenders need your business, so they try to make their terms attractive. However, when there are plenty of people trying to borrow a finite amount of money, lenders don't have to be as competitive, and their fees go up.

Some lenders offer mortgage loans for no points in order to attract business. Others offer lower interest rates but add on several points—sometimes three, four, or more. Try to achieve a balance between the interest rate and the points being charged when examining different financing options. Under current tax law, points are deductible for financing on the purchase of a principal residence. The following are examples of how much you can expect to pay in points:

	Mortgage Balance				
	$60,000	$70,000	$80,000	$90,000	$100,000
1 point	$ 600	$ 700	$ 800	$ 900	$1,000
2 points	1,200	1,400	1,600	1,800	2,000
3 points	1,800	2,100	2,400	2,700	3,000
4 points	2,400	2,800	3,200	3,600	4,000

Appraisal fee. This is the cost to the lender of hiring an independent

The Buyer's Closing Statement

Date:	November 1, 19___
Property:	112 B Street Elmwood, IL

(Buyer's name)

	Debits	Credits
Purchase price	$ 90,000.00	
Deposits to escrow		$ 11,962.43
Loan: First National Bank		82,000.00
Prorations 11/1 to 12/31:		
Property taxes	149.39	
Utilities	64.29	
Interest	768.75	
Title insurance	450.00	
Escrow fee	185.00	
Inspection report fee	260.00	
Notary fees	6.00	
Recording fees	26.00	
Loan fees	1,640.00	
Tax service fee	43.00	
Credit report	65.00	
Fire insurance (one year)	305.00	
Total	$93,962.43	$93,962.43

appraiser to determine the current market value of the home you are buying. It is passed on to you.

Transfer or assumption fee. This is a fee charged for processing the transfer of an existing mortgage loan from the seller to the buyer, if the mortgage is assumable.

Loan origination fee. This fee covers mortgage processing costs and is often 1 percent of the amount borrowed, but different from points. In some areas, this fee is paid at the time the mortgage is applied for and is not refundable (even if the loan is ultimately rejected).

Mortgage insurance. The lender might require that you take out a mortgage insurance policy, or you may ask for this coverage on your own. It is a form of life insurance that decreases as the balance on your mortgage decreases. It insures your life for the amount owed so that, in the event of your death, the mortgage loan is paid off.

A separate form of insurance required by some lenders and often called "mortgage insurance" is quite different. It is actually hazard insurance. It provides the lender protection in the event you default on your loan. If you stop making payments, the insurance company pays all or part of the balance to the lender. This type of insurance is normally required if your down payment is less than 20 percent of the equity in the home, and is included in your monthly payment. Although this coverage is for the lender's benefit, you pay the monthly premium.

Credit report fee. This fee is paid to an outside agency by the lender for a detailed report on your credit rating. It is sometimes charged to you at the time you apply for the loan, and is not refundable.

Survey fee. This fee is for a report showing the boundaries and exact location of the property. The lender may require the report if the property's legal description is not specific, or if the boundary is uncertain.

■ Fees for Title Service

Title search. Every mortgage, lien, and attachment on a piece of real estate is recorded in a local or county office and becomes part of the property's permanent record. A title search is the process of examining all recordings on one particular piece of property to make sure that there are no outstanding liens or claims against it that have not been disclosed. As the new owner, you become liable for all liens, which follow the property and not the person who was originally responsible. In some states, an attorney conducts the title search; in other states, a title company does the job.

Title insurance. This is an insurance policy that protects you in the event that the title search fails to turn up an outstanding and undisclosed lien. As long as that lien was recorded before you bought the property, you will not have to pay it; the title company assumes that risk in exchange for a one-time premium. The insurance remains in effect for as long as you own the property. Title insurance *can't* be transferred to anyone else.

Notary fee. This is a charge for certifying that an individual's signature is true, and is required on some of the documents you will sign at closing.

Recording fees. This is charged at the recorder's office (or office where documents are filed) for recording your deed and other documents.

Transfer tax. Some states and municipalities charge a tax for the transfer of property. It most often applies to the seller, but buyers may have to pay a tax as well.

■ Other Closing Costs

Attorney's fees. If you hire your own attorney, you will probably be required to settle up at closing, or shortly thereafter. If applicable, you will also be required to pay for the services of the attorney who managed the escrow process.

Escrow fees. In some states, the escrow company rather than an attorney handles the closing. They charge a fee for managing funds and documents.

Broker's commission. This is normally paid by the seller out of the proceeds of the sale. If you make special arrangements as part of the negotiated contract to pay part of the commission, you will be charged your share at closing.

Homeowner's insurance. Although not generally considered a closing cost, the lender will require proof that you have a valid, current policy. This protects you against fire, vandalism, other damages to the property, and liability for injuries to others. The first year's premium is often included as part of your closing costs.

Various lenders have their own procedures regarding closing costs, and the fees charged by local and state taxing authorities vary greatly from place to place. Your closing costs will reflect these distinctions. As a rule of thumb, you should expect to pay between 3 and 10 percent of the home's purchase price in closing costs. The largest variable is points.

Expect to receive a list of closing costs (including some that might not have been mentioned here). If you don't understand them, ask your real estate agent to explain them to you.

■ Prorating Expenses

One of the most confusing aspects of closing costs for many first-time buyers is prorating, or adjusting expenses between seller and buyer. The day you take title to your new home rarely corresponds exactly with the due dates of expenses such as utilities, fuel, property taxes, and interest payments for your mortgage loan. As the buyer, you will probably owe the seller money for these expenses for the period after the closing date for which the seller has already paid such expenses. Or an amount may be due that you will pay, part of which belongs to the seller.

The actual calculation can be done in one of three ways, depending on the type of expense:

1. It can be based on a 12-month scale, each month containing 30 days.

2. It can be based on a 365-day scale, with each day representing a percentage of the total number of actual days.

3. It can be computed monthly, based on the number of days the seller is responsible for and the number of days belonging to the buyer.

Prorating should be computed as accurately as possible and can be applied to several different expenses. The escrow agent will probably perform the calculations for you, but look them over to make sure no mistakes were made.

Let's say you take title to your new house on November 1 and property taxes have been prepaid through December 31. You will prorate your share of that expense as per the following examples (which all employ method 2, using actual number of days):

Total property tax bill	$450.62
Total period covered	July 1–December 31
Number of days in the period	184
Number of days from 11/1 to 12/31	61
Buyer's prorated share:	
61/184 x $450.62	= $149.39

If utility, water, or refuse bills are prepaid at a set amount, the daily rate can be computed:

Total water and refuse bill per quarter	$97.00
Days in current quarter 10/1 to 12/31	92
Daily cost of utilities ($97.00 / 92)	$1.054
Number of days from 11/1 to 12/31	61
Buyer's prorated share:	
61 x $1.054	= $64.29

When your closing date is different from the date when your first mortgage payment will be due, you will be charged interest for each day in between the two dates. If you close on November 1 and your first payment is due on December 1, you will be charged daily interest for those 30 days:

Mortgage balance	$82,000.00
Interest rate	11.25%
Interest, one year ($82,000 x 11.25%)	$ 9,225
Interest due for 30 days:	
30/360 x $9,225	= $ 768.75

Your lender might use a different method of calculation, so that actual interest charged may vary by a minor amount.

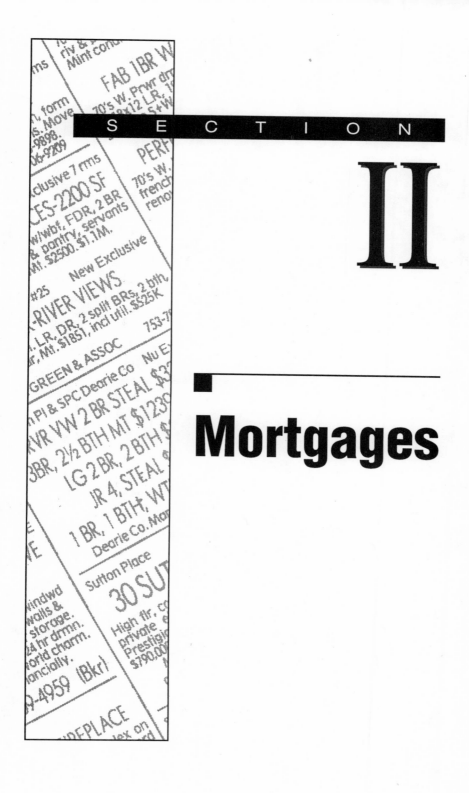

II

Mortgages

11

Shopping for a Mortgage

Finding the best possible mortgage financing for your new home requires some shopping around. You should become thoroughly familiar with both the range of choices available and the state of the current lending market.

This may be the single most important form of research you perform. So many home buyers spend hours negotiating to get a selling price down by two or three thousand dollars while ignoring the finer points of interest rates. For example, a one-quarter percent difference in your loan will make a significant difference over a 30-year period. Financing a $100,000 loan at 10.25 percent rather than at 10.5 percent will save $6,700 in interest.

Even when interest rates are moderate, there is no guarantee that they will remain that way. When rates start going up, changes seem to happen rapidly. There is no way to accurately predict the changes in future interest rates. Financial experts try to analyze economic factors influencing interest, but they are often wrong.

Like housing prices, the market for money is constantly affected by supply and demand. The interest rate and the interest you pay effect the rent charged for using (borrowing) the money. So, the supply and demand of money itself influences the interest rate. When money is tight—meaning too many people want to borrow and there is not enough money to satisfy everyone—the lender has a negotiating advantage, and rates are likely to be higher. The lender can then dictate terms, and the buyer has less flexibility in shopping around because all lenders' rates tend to be high at the same time.

Conversely, when money is not tight—when there is plenty of money available to lend, and relatively few people are seeking loans—lenders are more motivated to negotiate the interest rate and other terms, making it easier to shop around for a good bargain. At such times, you might be able to get an attractive rate and low points or a loan without any points at all.

■ Picking the Right Mortgage

To attract new customers, lenders sometimes offer inducements, including:

- Lower-than-current market interest rates.
- Loans with payments scheduled over exceptionally long terms.
- Rebates, discounts, and giveaways.

Each of these attention-getters deserves careful study. A lower interest rate, for example, might be good for only the first year. After that, the rate could take a drastic jump. Adjustable-rate mortgages often include this kind of "teaser" clause.

A loan with payments set over an exceptionally long term has two possible drawbacks. First of all, the longer your loan term, the lower your monthly payment, which seems attractive at first glance; but it also means more money going to pay off interest. Second, some loans may have a long-term payment schedule but call for the whole loan to be paid off in only a few years. That means you will have to come up with a lump sum to repay the whole loan or renegotiate the contract.

The length of time required to repay a loan is a very significant point to consider when shopping for mortgage financing. If you can afford the higher monthly payment, a 15-year mortgage is far cheaper than the more common 30-year mortgage. For instance, on a $100,000 loan at 10 percent interest, the 15-year loan payment will be $1,075 per month. This compares to payments of $878 per month for a 30-year loan at the same rate. The difference: $197. But by taking the higher monthly payment, you will save $122,499 in interest—not to mention paying off the loan in half the time. For those who can afford the extra monthly payment, this is a significant savings. A comparison of total interest costs between loans with 15-year and 30-year terms demonstrates the significance:

	TOTAL PAYMENTS *10% Loan*		
Mortgage	*30 Years*	*15 Years*	*Difference*
$ 75,000	$236,945	$145,073	$ 91,872
100,000	315,929	193,430	122,499
125,000	394,913	241,825	153,088
150,000	473,893	290,146	183,747

Note that in each example, the savings achieved with a shorter term is *greater* than the amount of the original loan. Additional savings are gained in another way: Lenders often will grant shorter-term loans at a lower interest rate.

Rebates, discounts, and giveaways are advertising gimmicks. When you are offered a cash rebate or discount, or a prize for applying for a mortgage, you can be sure that the cost of the giveaway is hidden in the lender's fees, or you're paying an interest rate calculated to make up the difference. Over the years, lenders have developed a variety of ways to make their offers sound like bargains in comparison with what their competitors are offering. Be especially careful of "creative" financing schemes; they are often nothing more than disguised high-cost loans. Remember, the lender is in the business of charging you interest; you are paying to use their money. Approaching a lender with that in mind will sharpen your skills in shopping for a fair and reasonable financing package.

■ Sources for Loans

You might feel the pressure and the complications of the buying process to the extent that you forget the all-important step of shopping for the best possible mortgage loan. Of all the bargaining you do, negotiating the best loan deal may provide the biggest savings.

The time spent shopping for a loan is invariably at least as important as the time spent looking at homes.

Be aware of these misconceptions when borrowing money to buy your home:

Misconception #1: You will be lucky to find a lender who will give you a loan at all.

The reality: Lenders are in the business of finding borrowers. That's you. If your credit history is clean and your income is high enough, you will be a valued customer for the bank.

Misconception #2: There aren't really any choices. All mortgage loans are the same.

The reality: You can get a low-cost loan the same way you can find good deals on food, appliances, cars, and anything else you buy. It requires shopping around.

Misconception #3: The real estate agent is an expert on mortgage financing and knows where to find the best deals.

The reality: Real estate agents are experts on selling homes. Of course, the best agents are skilled at finding loans for buyers, too, because without that, the whole deal can fall apart. The real estate agent might know, for example, where you can get a loan even if your credit is poor or your income is low. But those won't be the best deals. Don't count on the agent. Shop around on your own.

Finding a good mortgage loan is not a matter of luck. A reasonably priced mortgage loan can be negotiated. Explore all of your options. Remember, all loans are *not* the same; you might discover vast differences in terms, not only for interest rates, but for up-front costs as well. You really won't be able to tell which are the best deals until you make comparisons. It might take time, but considering how long you'll be making regular monthly payments, the time spent is an extremely worthwhile exercise.

Where should you start your search? It helps to know who grants the most loans. Lending sources include:

Savings and loan associations and banks. About seven out of every ten loans are made by these institutions, part of a growing trend. In 1980, only 55 percent of loans were generated from S&L's and banks.

A large segment of loans placed through these institutions are later sold to mortgage pools or trusts, which then sell shares to the public as investments. These pools are primarily operated or guaranteed by the federal government.

Builders and developers. When large tracts are developed, builders or developers often will lend money to buyers to sell properties quickly. They don't actually carry the loan, but make an agreement with a lender to act as middleman between buyer and lender. The developer sells or assigns each loan to the lender as homes sell.

Private loans. Some sellers will finance all or part of the purchase price of a house. However, these cases are rare. Most sellers want or need to get their money before they go on to their next home. Too often, when a seller offers to help a buyer with financing, it indicates that there is a problem with the house. The seller may be aware that the condition of the house might make it difficult for the buyer to get a commercial or government-sponsored loan. That means the buyer may have the same problem trying to sell it later.

Government agencies. Loans are offered through the Federal Housing Administration (FHA), the Veterans Administration (VA), the Farmers Home Administration (FmHA), and several smaller agencies. The trend in recent years is for these agencies to take on a smaller portion of total loans. For example, FHA made 16 percent of all loans in 1980. According to the U.S. Bureau of the Census and U.S. Department of Housing and Urban Development, as of 1993, FHA made only 9 percent of all loans; the VA went down during the same period from 8 percent to 6 percent; and FmHA carried only 1 percent of new loans, which was a third of their activity in 1980.

Mortgage brokers. These companies search for the best loans among several lending sources. This could be an efficient way to locate a competitive loan. A word of caution, however. Some brokers specialize in finding loans for people who have been turned down by local lenders, and that means you will have to pay higher fees and interest. Be certain the mortgage broker understands the terms you seek, your credit status, and the type of loan you want to get.

Terms and conditions vary by area, type of loan, type of lender, amount of the loan, and your credit. For example, the typical bank or savings and loan association requires that the proposed loan payment not exceed 28 percent of a borrower's gross monthly income. Government-insured or -guaranteed loans do not apply those standards.

Check the rules with each lender before prepaying any fees. To locate federal government agencies in your area that help with financing, check the government listing in your phone book.

The amount of financing activity in the United States is staggering. As of 1992, more than $3 trillion in borrowings was outstanding just for residential mortgages ($2.963 trillion for family homes). According to the Board of Governors of the Federal Reserve System, the breakdown of borrowed money by type of institution shows that mortgage pools and trusts account for nearly half of all loans.

Type of Institution	Amount in Billions	% of Total
Savings institutions	$ 490	17%
Mortgage pools or trusts	1,380	47
Commercial banks	508	17
Federal agencies	192	6
All other lenders	393	13
Total	$2,963	100%

■ Alternative Sources for Loans

The stronger your financial position—meaning the better your credit and the higher your income—the more financing choices you have. Lenders naturally prefer to do business with the most financially stable people. If you have limited funds for a down payment, your income is low, or you have had some credit problems in the past, you might not have many financing options. In extreme cases, you simply won't be able to find a loan until you resolve some of those problems.

You might have an easier time buying and financing a newly built home where the mortgage is part of the deal and is arranged through a developer or builder who may be looking to get all the homes sold as quickly as possible. Terms, though, will not be the best. The interest rate will be higher than the going commercial rate. And there is a chance the loan will be callable—the lender will have the right to demand full payment—in only a few years.

A suggestion: If your credit, income, or down payment make it difficult for you to qualify for a loan, look for a builder-sponsored deal and take it. But plan to replace it as soon as you can with another loan. You can refinance later and, in many respects, refinanced loans are easier to qualify for than original loans. From the lender's point of view, you are a better risk when you have been living in the home for some time. The refinance lender can check to see that all of your payments have been made on time, you have some equity in the home, and you have demonstrated your stability. If you are planning to refinance, be sure to keep your credit record clean. Make all mortgage payments on time, and be sure that all other payments are current as well. Even a single glitch on your credit report can ruin your chances for a better loan later.

Veterans may be able to get relatively fast approval for refinanced loans with attractive rates. About 2.1 million veterans and their spouses qualify for the Interest Rate Reduction Refinancing Loan program. For more information, call the VA at 800-827-1000.

You might also be able to get around the problem of qualification by assuming an existing loan. Some loans can be assumed with few or no requirements. If a seller has an assumable loan, it could be a good idea to assume the loan, especially if the interest rate is lower than the current going rate. However, some "assumable" loans specify that the lender has the right to raise the rate upon assumption, or to qualify the new buyer. (In these instances, the loan is not truly assumable, because all the terms can be renegotiated by the lender.)

■ The Mortgage Search Company

Until recently, the traditional way to find a loan was by pounding the pavement or by getting on the telephone. Now, mortgages can also be found via computer. The mortgage search company provides this service, often checking around the entire nation for the best deal available when you need it. The computer network is hooked up to hundreds of mortgage sources.

The mortgage search company agent, armed with a printout or a screen providing a wealth of alternatives, can quickly analyze your requirements, compared with your qualifications and limitations. The agent can match you up with the best potential lending sources for your particular situation. This service can be well worth the fee, because unlikely sources can be quickly eliminated, often on the basis that you simply don't meet lenders' initial qualifications. This can save time, energy, and perhaps a lot of money as well.

■ Other Considerations

Choosing the right mortgage means being aware of more than just the interest rate. Here are some of the other variables to remember:

Points. A comparison between lenders is difficult when both the interest rate and the number of points are different. (A point, equal to 1 percent of the loan amount, is a substantial expense that may be added to closing costs and is payable at closing, or it can be added to the amount financed, depending on the lender's policies.) For example, let's say that Lender A wants to charge 10 percent on a $100,000 loan and also charges two points, or $2,000. The monthly payment is $877.58 on a 30-year term. Lender B charges 10.25 percent but charges no points. The monthly payment will be $896.11 on a 30-year term. The comparison between these two lenders, without considering additional interest costs, follows:

	Lender A	*Lender B*	*Difference*
Monthly payment	$ 877.58	$ 896.11	$ 18.53
Points	$2,000.00	0	$2,000.00
Number of months to make up the difference:		$2,000.00/$18.53 = 108 months	

It would take nine years to make up the difference between these two options. What this means is that Lender A offers a better deal if you intend to stay in the home for more than nine years. (The average first-time buyer stays less than five years.) Also, don't forget that if the lender adds the points to your borrowings, you will have to pay compounded interest on the amount of the points. You should also think about what you could earn if you paid no points and invested the $2,000 for nine years. The comparison is complex, but these questions should be kept in mind when trying to decide between alternatives.

Type of mortgage. Another consideration is the type of mortgage for which you're applying. A 15-year repayment term involves higher monthly payments but substantially less interest. The savings you achieve with a 15-year term over a 30-year term are *higher* than the full amount of the loan itself. Example: At 10 percent on a $100,000 loan, total payments on the 30-year term are $315,929. Payments on a 15-year term add up to $193,430. The difference is $122,499—greater than the loan of $100,000.

Prepaying the mortgage. Accelerating your mortgage payments can save a lot of money. For example, you might agree to a 30-year loan because you're not sure you can afford the higher monthly payments required of a 15-year loan. Furthermore, you might not even qualify for a 15-year loan, since qualification is based on a comparison between your monthly income and the proposed monthly payment. In this situation, you can still save a lot of money by prepaying part of the mortgage each month. You could agree to the 30-year repayment term but make payments at the 15-year rate. The result: You will save a lot in interest payments and pay off the loan in half the time. In addition, if you need to suspend the accelerated payments for a while, you can do so without penalty.

■ The Lender's Decision

How do lenders decide whether to accept or reject your application for a mortgage loan? It is not an arbitrary decision, although it may appear to be so to first-time buyers. You should know that lenders are forbidden by law to discriminate against applicants on the basis of race, sex, age, or other protected status. If your application is rejected, you will be given a reason for the decision. The process of evaluation and investigation by the lender is very thorough, and is designed to ensure that the lender's risks are minimized.

The lender is concerned about your qualifications because they want to ensure that you can afford the monthly payments. They judge you on your income, of course, but they also look at the length of time you've been living at your current address, length of employment, and of course, your credit history. If you appear to be financially unstable, especially if you have not kept up with other payments, your application will not be favorably viewed by the lender. In comparison, if you are financially stable and have excellent credit, you have a better chance.

Some lenders are more flexible than others. In a small town, a local lender is intimately familiar with the area's real estate market as well as with the people. Being personally acquainted with a banker certainly doesn't hurt (unless you were high school rivals, of course). A small-town banker also knows the local real estate agents, and might be willing to underwrite mortgage loans that would be turned down by a larger bank in a major city. There, the application procedure is understandably impersonal.

Some banks are willing to carry a mortgage as a "portfolio loan." That means the bank actually puts up the money and keeps the loan on their books. The more common practice is to grant the loan under strict federal guidelines and then transfer the balance to one of the big government pools. This enables the bank to get its money back and loan it out again to someone else, effectively making the bank a transfer agent for the federal government. (You get the loan, the bank puts up the money, and the mortgage pool takes it over.) With the widespread activity of the Government National Mortgage Association (Ginnie Mae) and the Federal National Mortgage Association (Fannie Mae), this is a common transaction. The lender usually continues to collect monthly payments and administer impound funds for insurance and taxes, but the market is predominantly managed through investment pools.

The lender has to comply with the federal rules imposed by the pools if they want to qualify for transferring the debt out of the bank. Even lenders who carry portfolio loans will usually not be willing to finance more than 80 percent of the purchase price, although many programs will allow up to 90 percent financing. FHA and VA programs often allow borrowers to pay little or no down payment.

Before granting you a loan, the lender will check your record as well as the property itself. In particular, the lender will look carefully at the following:

The neighborhood. The lender evaluates the neighborhood and its characteristics as part of its risk assessment. Just as lenders are forbidden by law to discriminate against certain protected personal classes, they also cannot reject a loan merely because of where the property is located. However, the condition of the neighborhood affects current and future property values and indicates the kind of borrower and homeowner you are likely to be. If there has been a high level of development activity and people want to move to an area, that tells the lender that the demand for homes in that neighborhood is high. However, if the neighborhood is characterized by several abandoned homes and empty lots, and the rate of foreclosures is high, the desirability of the area is obviously much lower. The lender is also interested in the percentage of housing that is owner-occupied versus the percentage that is rented out. From the lender's point of view, the higher the rate of owner-occupied housing, the better. Neighborhoods with high owner-occupied rates tend to have better-maintained homes that tend to increase in value more than homes in rental neighborhoods.

The house. Before granting a mortgage loan for any property, the lender will insist on obtaining an independent appraisal. While they maintain the right to choose the appraiser, you will get the bill. Most lenders will expect the appraisal report fee to be paid up-front. Appraisers consider a house's overall condition, its size and location, the shape of the lot, number and size of rooms, energy efficiency, landscaping, and conformity—how well the house fits into the neighborhood. This means that all the houses should be approximately the same size, preferably of similar design, on lots of about the same size, and of similar or identical age. Although conformity does not make a particular house very interesting, it does contribute to its value. Even an exceptionally nice house—one that is larger, newer, or sits on a bigger lot—has a limited market value because of the problems of conformity. Appraisers also look for other negatives such as erosion, poor drainage, evidence of past flooding, safety hazards, and obsolete heating systems, to name a few. To the degree that a house and its systems are out of date, the appraiser's estimate will be reduced for obsolescence.

Your credit rating. Another fee the lender will probably expect you to pay up front is the fee to get a credit report. In order to determine your personal financial history, the lender contacts one of the three national reporting agencies or a local branch office, pays a fee, and gets a detailed rundown on your credit: outstanding loans, credit and store cards, lines of credit, and, most important of all, whether you have ever been more than 30 days late on your payments. The report also includes any judgments or liens against you and your property, previous bankruptcies or foreclosures, bad debts, and other important financial data. You should probably get a copy of your credit report from each of the three national agencies before even applying for credit, just to see if there are any unexpected surprises awaiting you. Agencies sometimes make mistakes. If your credit profile is incorrect, you should write to the credit reporting companies and have any mistakes taken off their reports to avoid trouble with your loan application. Whenever you are rejected for credit, you are entitled to a free copy of your credit report (if you apply for it in writing within a specified time limit).

Employment and assets. Lenders will also verify your dates of employment and level of salary. The lender will also ask you to list on the application form all your assets, including bank accounts, investments, current value of automobiles, furniture, clothing, jewelry, art, and net worth in a business; liabilities such as current balances on credit cards, outstanding auto and personal loans, and alimony; and sources of income, including salaries, investments, business income, alimony, and annuities. Lenders look for the right combination of income, assets and liabilities, and credit history.

■ Income and Employment Profile

To be a successful loan applicant, you need a steady income large enough to support the monthly mortgage payment. Lenders are basically interested in borrowers with one primary income supported by a secondary income. Primary income includes regularly paid wages, whereas secondary income includes commissions, bonuses, tips, and overtime pay. Consistency in your earning record, from both primary and secondary sources, is vitally important. How else can the lender judge your ability to pay? If you have been at your current job for two years or more, you're more qualified for a loan than someone who has been employed for only a few months.

If you are self-employed, be prepared to give the lender a current balance sheet and income statement, and copies of at least two years of your income tax returns (some lenders will ask for three years), as well as copies of your business bank accounts for the past year.

As a general rule, lenders require that your total monthly mortgage payment does not exceed a set percentage of your gross income (income before taxes and other deductions are subtracted). The mortgage payment not only includes principal and interest but also payments for taxes and homeowner's insurance as well. Most lenders also look at utility bills and any long-term debt payments for which you are obligated, in addition to the monthly mortgage payment. Can you afford the mortgage payment considering your other obligations and your income? That is always the central question. As long as the total of all committed payments does not exceed an established percentage of your gross income, you may qualify based on that lender's standards. (In general, lenders have a degree of flexibility.)

Before applying to a lender for a loan, ask what is needed for qualification. You will probably be able to figure out whether you qualify on your own, even before putting in an application. Another good reason for asking for this information is to figure out what you can afford. By first calculating the maximum mortgage for which you are qualified, you will know how much you will need for a down payment; you will also know the maximum price you can afford to pay for a house.

■ Debt Management

Lenders want to see a clean credit history without any of these big problems: foreclosures, bankruptcies, or liens against property you own. A clean credit history is the mark of a mature person who understands the importance of managing personal finances responsibly—a starting point for just about any lender.

Lenders will look for signs of bad credit. For example, if your credit report shows one or more debts that you did not list on your credit application, lenders may think you're trying to hide something. Take great care in filling out loan forms. List all credit information with the understanding that the bank *will* check everything and, if anything is left off, they *will* find out about it.

If you have had a bankruptcy or foreclosure, you can expect the bank to ask for signs of improved financial performance. Lenders will almost certainly reject an application if you have a consistent problem with credit, even without a bankruptcy or foreclosure. The more recent the problems, the worse for you, and the more skeptical the lender will be. That's why recent credit history is important and why lenders look at it so carefully.

If your credit report lists any problems, lenders will give you the opportunity to explain them in writing. If there is an error, include paid bills and canceled checks as proof to the lender that the credit agency or a reporting company has made a mistake. And don't forget to also send the information to the credit agency so the error can be removed from your file.

If you have good credit—for example, multiple charge cards—that's a sign that other lenders have faith in your ability to repay debts. However, some lenders may be reluctant to lend money to someone with too many cards because they fear borrowers may be overextended. If you accumulate debt without an accompanying growth in your personal net worth—assets (cars, real estate, and cash) minus liabilities (loans and outstanding balances on credit cards)—then a lender might believe that your level of consumer debt is dangerously high. In this situation, adding the high mortgage debt could jeopardize your ability to repay the loan. A lender might ask you to cancel some of your credit cards to qualify, which might be a good idea.

You will be asked to supply the lender with proof of your viable net worth or evidence that you have the means for building one. Again, the demonstration of a steady work history, responsible credit management, and some cash for a down payment all help to make this point convincingly.

Lenders also compare "liquid" and "nonliquid" assets. Liquid assets are cash, investments you can access, money other people owe to you—in short, any asset that can be converted to cash in a short period of time. Nonliquid assets include real estate, investments committed or locked away for the future, furniture, art work—anything that you probably cannot convert into cash very quickly.

Liabilities have characteristics similar to assets. Any liability that has to be paid off in the near future is called a short-term or current liability. These include credit card balances and 12-month payment plans on any current loans. Long-term liabilities are loan balances beyond 12-month payment plans. Lenders like to compare current assets and current liabilities to see how you invest and manage cash. Lenders also look for some liquidity in the form of savings, for example—money you can get your hands on if an emergency arises.

Aside from these financial tests and relationships, you need to look for a lender who is willing to help you through the application process. Such a lender can be an enormous help in getting a loan. A conscientious loan officer will work with you and ensure that the financial commitment is completely understood, so you can avoid the ultimate disaster—losing your home because you can't keep up with the mortgage payments—which is a loss to everyone, you as well as the bank. Lenders prefer not to have to foreclose. It's expensive, and it means the bank has to try to find another buyer for the home. Bankers would rather be in the money business, not the real estate business.

12

Interest and Mortgages

Lending money is a business like any other. Money is the product and lenders are selling that product to their customers (borrowers). Lenders "buy" and "sell" money (to make a profit), assume risks, and occasionally lose money on a transaction. If you approach the borrowing process with this point of view in mind, you will have a better-than-average grasp of how the lender will look at you as a potential borrower.

Interest rates dictate the lending market. For that reason, it's also fair to say that interest rates control the real estate market. If rates are so high that the majority of first-time buyers cannot qualify, there is no market. In such markets, the price of real estate does not matter as much as the financing terms a buyer can meet. Not only do rates affect the home buyer, they also affect the lender. Every institution has to adjust its rates according to what it has to pay for money. Just as a grocery store raises the price of produce when its wholesale prices rise, lenders raise the interest rate when its wholesale money supply cost goes up.

Where do lenders get money? One source is savings depositors. Lenders such as savings and loan associations, banks, and credit unions encourage their customers to place money in savings accounts or money market accounts. That money is then loaned out to other customers who want to borrow money. The rate the lender charges for its loans is higher than the rate it pays to depositors. The difference, called the "spread," enables the institution to pay its operating expenses (salaries, office expenses, insurance, rent, etc.) and to make a profit.

If you have ever watched the interest market, you know that rates are changing all the time. The reasons interest rates go up and down are complex. Many factors influence rates, not only banking and financial markets at home, but in other countries as well.

Interest rates change according to the principles of supply and demand. The more money there is to lend, the lower the rate of interest. And the less money, the higher the rate of interest. If too many people want to borrow a limited amount of money, that demand will push up the rates; if too few people want to borrow, the lack of demand will force rates down.

Lenders charge different rates of interest for newly built homes and older homes. Older-home loans are lower because there is virtually no depreciation of the materials and systems. Therefore, risks are reduced when lenders work with buyers of brand new homes.

Figure 12.1 Decline in Mortgage Balance

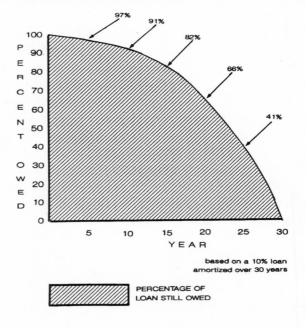

based on a 10% loan
amortized over 30 years

PERCENTAGE OF
LOAN STILL OWED

■ Computing Interest

Lenders normally compute interest according to an established standard. A loan should be a "fully amortized," or periodically reduced, loan. If a lender, either an institution or individual, uses another method of computing interest, it could mean trouble. Before you agree to any financing, be sure that you thoroughly understand how interest is computed.

With the commonly used fully amortized interest method, each monthly payment is divided between interest and principal (the repayment amount). The monthly payment is calculated to repay the loan in full by a specified period of time. The shorter the repayment period, the higher your payments.

A word of caution: One form of "creative" financing involves setting monthly payments to amortize the loan over a 30-year payment period. However, the loan is due and payable in five years. This means you will need a large amount of cash, or you'll have to refinance when that loan comes due. This type of contract does *not* run for the 30-year period; it is only amortized on the 30-year schedule. What it really means is your payments will be almost all interest. Let's say your mortgage is for $100,000, and the interest rate is 10 percent. Monthly payments set on the 30-year schedule are $877.58. However, the loan is due after five years. At that time, you will still owe $96,573.63. Your total payments of $52,654.80 will consist of only $3,426.37 in repayment of the loan and $49,228.43 in interest. (See the following table.)

End of Month	Monthly Payments of $877.58	Interest	Principal	Balance ($100,000)
12	$10,530.96	$ 9,974.96	$ 556.00	$99,444.00
24	10,530.96	9,916.75	614.21	98,829.79
36	10,530.96	9,852.42	678.54	98,151.25
48	10,530.96	9,781.39	749.57	97,401.68
60	10,530.96	9,702.91	828.05	96,573.63
Total	$52,654.80	$49,228.43	$3,426.37	—

Interest costs are, indeed, high. If your 30-year loan ran the whole period using the same terms above, your total payments would be $315,929 ($877.58 x 360 months), of which $215,929 ($315,929 - $100,000) would be interest.

Based on the aforementioned example, you would pay for the mortgage three times over if the mortgage ran 30 years. Why is the interest cost so high? The answer is found in the way the monthly payment is broken down. The *rate* of interest you pay is an annual rate, and you pay one-twelfth of that against the outstanding loan balance each month. Therefore, in the earlier years of the loan term, when the balance is high, more of the total payment will go toward interest. In the later years, when the balance is lower, more of the payment goes toward principal.

Using the 10 percent example on a $100,000 loan running 30 years, the monthly payment is $877.58. How is the interest on that payment actually calculated? The following is the step-by-step breakdown for the first month's payment on a $100,000 loan:

Step 1: Multiply the outstanding loan balance by the interest rate to get the preliminary interest: $100,000.00 x 10.0% = $10,000.00

Step 2: Divide the preliminary interest by 12 to get this month's interest: $10,000.00 / 12 = $833.33

Step 3: Subtract the first month's interest from the total payment to find out how much is going toward principal: $877.58 - $833.33 = $44.25

Step 4: Subtract the first month's payment of principal from the beginning loan balance to find the new loan outstanding balance: $100,000.00 - $44.25 = $99,955.75

As you can see, in the first month, out of a payment of $877.58, only $44.25 goes toward paying the loan. Of course, many years later when the loan balance is lower, more of the payment will go toward principal. For example, when the loan balance is down to about $20,000, interest will be only about $167 per month, meaning that more than $700 per month will be applied against the loan balance. The rate of decline in the loan's balance will have grown.

Figure 12.1 on page 102 shows how, during the early years of a 10 percent loan, the principal balance declines slowly, and during the later years, how the rate of decline accelerates.

∎ The Mortgage

A mortgage is a claim against property. When you buy a home and get a mortgage, you are essentially pledging to either repay the loan or allow the lender to take back the property and sell it in order to recapture the money you were loaned. In other words, your home is collateral for the loan. If you don't keep up your payments, the lender has the right to foreclose and take the home away.

Foreclosures are unusual events. Many homeowners fall behind on payments by a month or two, eventually making up the difference. Lenders will not file for foreclosure until it becomes clear that a borrower is defaulting on the loan. A far more common problem for homeowners is the effect that late payments have on credit ratings. If you are more than 30 days late on a payment, it shows up on your credit report and remains there for seven years.

You will probably finance the majority of your home's cost through a lending institution. Make sure you pay your monthly payment on time without fail. Be aware that the lender will charge a late fee if you miss the due date. If you later apply for credit and your lender is asked whether you make payments on time, any tardy months will be reported, and it could mean a credit application will be rejected.

Total financing on your home may consist of a combination of methods. The three ways to finance a purchase are:

1. Cash. You will almost always be required to put up 10 to 20 percent of the purchase price.

2. Institutional loans. A conventional or government-insured or guaranteed loan is the most popular ways to get financing. You will either get your own loan or assume an existing loan.

3. A private mortgage. The seller carries part (or all) of the amount financed, or you get a second mortgage from a relative, a friend, or an investor. The second mortgage is so called because the institution holding the first mortgage gets paid first if you default; the second mortgage is next in order of priority to be repaid. That mortgage's interest rate is usually higher than the institutional rate charged on a first mortgage, for the reason that it has secondary priority for repayment in the event of default.

Some lenders will grant a loan of 80 percent of the purchase price, or in some cases 90 or even 95 percent. However, they do insist that you put up the balance in most situations. The lender wants to ensure that you have something at stake; otherwise, what's to prevent you from simply walking away from the deal if you decide you don't want the home anymore? Your down payment tells the lender that you are a serious borrower. If you borrow 80 percent of the purchase price, the lender will expect you to come up with the difference in cash, or at least most of it.

■ Fixed Versus Adjustable-Rate Loans

Loans from conventional sources—usually savings and loan associations, banks, credit unions, and similar institutions—will have either a fixed rate of interest for the entire loan term or an adjustable rate, meaning the rate can change.

Depending on your circumstances, one type of loan may be preferable to the other. However, it isn't possible to say that one type is *always* better, because everyone's needs are different. For example, the amount of time you plan to live in a home may dictate whether one form of financing is better than the other. As a rule, most first-time home buyers move on within five years. Therefore, locking yourself into a long-term rate doesn't always make sense.

How do the two types of mortgages work? A *fixed-rate* mortgage means just that: The rate of interest is established by contract, and it will never change. No matter what happens to market rates, if the lender grants you a fixed rate, you pay that rate until one of three things occurs: You sell the home, you refinance, or you reach the end of the loan term. The newer and more innovative adjustable-rate mortgage (ARM) specifies that, if market interest rates go up, so will *your* rate and *your* monthly payment. And if market interest rates go down, your rate should go down as well. However, if the lender's timing of rate increases was delayed by the terms of the contract, your rate probably won't decline until the difference is made up.

The ARM contract spells out how and when increases are applied. Typically, the index rate is reviewed only once or twice per year, and adjustments are applied on a delayed basis. For example, the index change as of September 30 might be used to increase interest rates effective the following January.

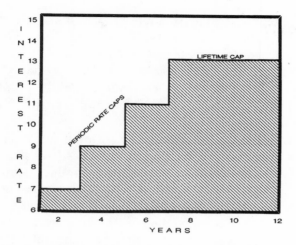

Figure 12.2 Adjustable Rate Mortgage Caps

The ARM first came into being as a way to help people qualify for loans whose incomes were too low to get fixed-rate terms. The original ARM (developed in the late 1970s) started out with a fairly low rate and payment, with a contractual provision that after a year or two, the rate would jump—and the monthly payment would follow suit.

Note: The change in ARM rates is set according to the index rate spelled out in the loan contract. If that index rate goes up, your ARM rate will be increased by the same percentage. The most commonly used index for ARM contracts is the one-year constant-maturity Treasury index (a rate applied to financing a part of the national debt). On the West Coast, many lenders prefer using the 11th District Cost of Funds Index (COFI).

ARM contracts really caught on during the early 1980s, when exceptionally high interest rates shut the majority of people out of the housing market except those with very high incomes or very large down payments. Since then, the ARM has evolved into a widely used method for qualifying people to buy their first home.

Understandably, when extremely high interest rates ruled, many people opted for ARM contracts. By the end of 1984, according to the Federal National Mortgage Association, more than half of all new mortgage loans were arranged by way of ARMs. Since then, mortgage interest rates have dropped. Currently, about one in five new mortgages has an adjustable rate. That means that when people think about long-term plans, they think of a fixed rate of interest and the benefits of being able to predict what their housing will cost. Even if the interest rate and payment are slightly higher for a fixed rate than for the ARM, about four out of five new home buyers want that predictability.

The exception to this nationwide rule is in California, where high prices still force home buyers to look for ways to qualify. There, one-third of all home loans are ARMs.

The appeal of the ARM is in the initial lower rate offered by the lender, who wants the flexibility of raising rates later should market rates rise. For the privilege of locking in rates for three decades with a fixed-rate mortgage loan, you will have to pay a higher rate. A comparison between ARM and fixed-rate loans is complicated by the fact that future rate changes cannot be known. Some lenders offer you a computerized comparison assuming that maximum rate increases are applied. Always ask for such a comparison.

With a book of interest amortization tables, you can construct your own comparison chart. Example: You are comparing two loans. One is a fixed-rate loan at 10 percent. The other starts at 7 percent, with potential increases of no more than 1 percent per year, with a maximum of 5 percent in overall rate increases (loan amount is $100,000).

Through Year	Fixed-Rate	Total Payments (Percent)	ARM
1	$ 10,531	7	$ 9,304
2	21,062	8	18,566
3	31,593	9	28,222
4	42,124	10	38,753
5	52,655	11	50,181
6	61,186	12	62,524
7	73,717	12	74,867
8	84,248	12	87,210
9	94,779	12	99,553
10	105,310	12	111,896

Note: This example compares total payments, which include both interest and principal. For most families, interest costs are not as critical as total monthly payments. However, a lender should be able to provide you with a breakdown of total payments *and* overall interest costs on a comparative basis.

You can see by the chart that after the sixth year, the ARM becomes increasingly expensive. However, this is only one example. Ask your lender to calculate an exact "worst-case" comparison for you. A comparison can help you make an informed decision. For example, if you plan to sell your home within the first six years (most first-time buyers do), the ARM is a more sensible choice.

Keep these important points in mind if you are considering the ARM:

- The ARM might be necessary just to qualify for a loan. Remember, the lender compares the proposed mortgage payment to your income. Higher interest rates require higher monthly payments. If the higher rates on a fixed-rate mortgage will make it difficult for you to make your monthly payments, the lender will simply reject your application.
- Even if the rate goes up in the future, your income is likely to keep pace. We all expect to make more money in the future, and as a rule, as we gain experience and work skills, that expectation comes true. A good way to think about ARM payments is in comparison to income. If the ARM payment represents 23 percent of your income, but it increases, what is the new ARM percentage? As long as it's still at or below 23 percent of your income, the relative burden of the mortgage remains the same.
- You can refinance in the future. Whether an ARM's rates go up or not, you might consider refinancing. That idea is especially good when interest rates are fairly low, and when lenders are competing for business—meaning low points are being charged, for example. That's the time to lock in a competitive fixed-rate contract.
- ARM contracts include safeguards that at least limit the pace and amount of increase you can be charged.

There are three types of "caps" involved:

First, the contract will specify that rates can be increased only at predetermined intervals. For example, an ARM contract might state that interest rates can be increased only once every year or every two years.

Second, the amount of the periodic increase will be limited. For example, the contract may state that you will never be subjected to an increase greater than 2 percent at one time.

Third, the contract will spell out a "lifetime" cap, meaning that over the entire extent of the mortgage period, you will never have to pay interest above a specified number of points. For example, you might enter an ARM contract beginning with an interest rate of 7 percent. The contract might specify that the lifetime cap is 6 additional percentage points, meaning the maximum rate you will ever have to pay will be 13 percent.

All of these specific terms have to be included in the ARM contract. The mistake too many people make is picking a mortgage based on what they read in a lender's advertisements or brochures. Sit down with the loan officer and ask questions such as:

- Can you give me a detailed comparison between ARM and fixed-rate loans for the first 10 years?
- Can you break down the comparison to show total payments *and* their interest?
- Does the contract allow me to convert to a fixed rate in the future? What conversion fees, if any, are involved?
- How often does the institution review and adjust rates?
- What is the maximum periodic cap?
- What is the maximum lifetime cap?
- What index is used in calculating rate changes?
- Will the rate fall if the index also falls? How is that calculated, and what is the minimum interest charged?
- Does the contract allow prepayment of principal?

The combination of periodic rate caps and the lifetime cap in the ARM is illustrated in Figure 12.2 on page 107.

■ Selecting the Best Loan

Deciding whether to ask for a fixed-rate loan or an adjustable-rate loan depends on your particular circumstances, how much you have for a down payment, monthly income, and how long you believe you will remain in that home. In addition, assuming you can qualify for either type of loan, you need to decide how much financial risk you're willing to take. Some people are willing to pay more in exchange for absolute predictability.

In judging your personal circumstances, you need to factor in what will happen to your family in the next few years. Are you buying a small house because you don't have any children? If so, it is possible you'll have children soon and outgrow that house? If you think it likely that you'll want to trade up in a few years, an ARM will probably be a better way to go. However, if you are certain that you won't be moving in the near future because you're secure in your job and the house will be large enough for your plans, you will probably prefer locking in a long-term rate. Go with a fixed-rate mortgage.

The amount of your down payment will also determine which type of mortgage you choose. The higher your down payment, the more flexibility you have in picking a mortgage and the more likely you are to qualify for a wider range of loan options. For example, if you are selling a previously owned house and will be using your equity for a large down payment, you have more flexibility. You can pick a loan based on the number of points, rate comparisons, and equity.

Your income is always the most determining factor in picking a loan. If you are just barely able to qualify for an ARM and nothing else, the debate is academic—but you might want to look at the question again in the future, when your income is higher, especially if rates are down. You might then want to exchange your ARM for a refinanced fixed-rate mortgage, lowering your monthly payments and getting around the initial qualification problems.

How long do you plan to stay in a home? You cannot really know the answer to this one, but you can make an estimate based on what you currently know. Is it likely that you will relocate to change jobs? Would you prefer to live elsewhere? Or are you in the community for the long term, and have no intentions of leaving?

Finally, how much risk can you afford to take? This is what financial professionals call risk tolerance—your willingness to take a chance in order to reduce costs, versus the need for predictability and a willingness to pay more to get it. You need to identify how much risk tolerance you and your spouse have before deciding where to shop for mortgages.

■ Total Interest Expense

The type of mortgage loan you select will have a definite effect on the amount of interest you end up paying. Over the lifetime of a 30-year loan, the interest will exceed the total amount you borrow. With a 15-year mortgage, you cut the interest considerably, but the monthly payment is higher, too.

With a fixed-rate loan, you need to be aware of the market rates. If those rates are lower than what you're paying, you may consider refinancing with a new, fixed-rate mortgage or with an ARM. The decision should be based on the prevailing rates, your personal plans, and the time remaining on your loan. If market interest rates remain below your rate (especially if they drop even further), it's time to think about replacing your loan.

Expect to pay fees like points and processing fees for the new loan, and probably for a new appraisal, too. It's worth it, though, if your interest savings justify it. There is a way to determine whether or not you will profit from refinancing: by calculating your "break-even" point on the cost of refinancing, and then comparing that to how long you plan to keep the home.

Here's how it works. Let's say that your current mortgage payment is $877 per month. You choose to refinance because rates have dropped. You are told that your new payment will be $805 per month, or $72 lower per month. After asking for an estimate of closing costs (you are told that those costs will be about $2,000), divide the closing costs by the monthly savings:

$2,000.00 / $72 = 27.8

It will take you about 28 months to cover the cost of getting a new loan. In other words, you save $72 per month, but it will cost $2,000 to refinance. As long as you plan to remain in that home for more than 28 months, it is worth refinancing. However, if you are thinking of trading up and getting a bigger home soon, why go to the expense of refinancing?

An ARM contract is often refinanced with the same kind of comparison in mind. If your lender increases your monthly payment by $150, you might decide it's time to go mortgage shopping again. In fact, many first-time buyers sign ARM contracts—often because that's all they qualify for—with the intention of later replacing the ARM with a lower-cost, fixed-rate mortgage at a time when rates are lower, lenders are more liberal with their terms, and refinancing will be easier. Remember, though, that if rates are rising in an ARM contract, it usually means the whole market is rising as well. If ARM rates are up, it probably also means that all interest rates, including those on fixed-rate loans, are up.

For example, if you start out with an ARM at 8½ percent interest, and fixed rates are running at about 10 percent, you're ahead of the game. On a $100,000 loan with a 30-year term, you're saving about $109 per month. But if your contract has a ceiling of 14 percent and you reach that level several years later, monthly payments could climb a staggering $416 above their original level, a 54 percent increase. At the same time, you might discover that fixed rates on other mortgages have followed suit. (Remember, the ARM is convenient, cheap at first, and easy to qualify for, but you also assume risks.)

Sometimes, interest rates climb too high too quickly, and people simply stop buying homes. They can't qualify for mortgages, which creates a dilemma for lenders. A shortage of qualified buyers means no business. It's as though a produce market, due to flooding, was forced to charge $15 per pound for apples. Very few customers would be willing to pay those prices, so the market would dwindle.

When that happens in the real estate market, lenders try to find creative ways to help people buy homes. But that may mean problems for borrowers later on. For example, lenders may approve interest-only loans, with a clause calling for repayment of the *full* amount of the loan in five years, maybe less. This is called a balloon payment. But if you're paying interest only, you might as well be paying rent. At least then, the landlord is responsible for fixing anything that breaks down.

In some markets, lenders and buyers justify balloon payments with the argument that market values can rise enough to justify their use. It enables otherwise unqualified buyers to take part in the market. Unfortunately, the reality is that many people who try to get into the housing market in this way end up losing their homes, along with the payments they've made. There is no way to tell if market values will rise, and the past is not a dependable indicator. There is the additional risk that, when the loan comes due, you won't be able to refinance it, forcing you to give up the property.

▪ Pros and Cons of ARMs

The ARM features an interest rate that changes if and when a related index of interest rates changes. The index, timing, and limitations of the change are all spelled out in the ARM contract. You should make sure you understand all of the terms before signing any documents.

In the approximate period covering 1979 to 1981, interest rates were at unprecedented highs—at or above 20 percent. The housing market was in bad shape and virtually all financed mortgages involved some very creative ideas, most based on deferring principal payments. In that atmosphere, the ARM contract caught on and survived.

During that time, lenders took on many mortgages that had been written years before, at relatively low rates: 5, 6, and 7 percent. Meanwhile, they were paying depositors higher rates. The creation of the ARM by lenders was intended to close the gap between their cost of money (what they had to pay to borrow and what savings accounts earned) and what they could get at market rates (interest on loans). The long-term fixed mortgage became a big problem for lenders, and many, especially savings and loan associations, suffered large losses.

If you are among those first-time buyers who cannot qualify for a fixed-rate loan because of your income level, you will probably end up with an ARM contract. If that makes you uncomfortable, shop for other lender terms. There may be a loan package out there just right for you. For example, some lenders offer ARM contracts with a stipulation that you can convert to a fixed-rate mortgage at any time within the first few years (usually three to five years). As long as the fixed-rate interest is not much higher than what you are paying on the ARM contract, converting is a simple matter. In this way, you can qualify for an ARM, get the loan, and then convert to the contract you really want.

Some lenders also offer ARM contracts with down-payment requirements below those of fixed-rate mortgages. With lower risks for lenders, the policies and terms for these ARMs may be more liberal.

The major disadvantage of the ARM contract is that you have no way of knowing for certain what your payments are going to be in the future. As rates climb, so do your payments. This increase can be fairly large if your payments rise at the maximum allowed by the ARM contract.

For example, you might start out with an $80,000 loan in an ARM contract at 8½ percent, payable over 30 years. But suppose the maximum cap is 14 percent:

Rate	Monthly Payment
8½	$615.13
9	643.70
10	702.06
11	761.86
12	822.89
13	884.96
14	947.90

The difference of roughly $60 per month for each percentage point adds up to an overall increase ranging from about $615 per month to $948, about 54 percent higher than the starting point. Growing interest costs translate to a higher overall cost for your home.

■ Rate and Payment Caps

Rate and payment caps limit the rate of increased expense you will experience in your ARM contract. But some of these caps don't protect you; instead, they protect the lender. The three limitations in the contract are:

1. A limitation on the frequency of rate increases. The lender agrees by contract that your interest rate will be reviewed once per year, once per two years, or at some other specific interval.

2. A cap on the annual increase. Limiting the amount of additional interest you can be charged each year controls the rate of growth in your monthly payments. For example, a contract might specify that the lender cannot exceed a growth rate more than one percentage point per year. When the index-based calculation exceeds that restriction, the lender usually has the right to carry the increase over to the following year. An exception to this cap could be the initial rate increase in the second or third year. Some lenders sell ARMs at extremely low or "teaser" rates, and then jump the rate up to market rates after one or two years.

3. A cap on overall expense. This sets a specific limit on the overall total interest you can be charged over the entire contract period. It will be expressed either as a percentage rate or the number of points above the beginning interest rate.

Generally, these limitations are good protection for you. They give some certainty to your long-term mortgage. However, it isn't always that simple. The following example shows how some of these limitations can work against you. Let's say your contract specifies that your interest rate can never exceed 14 percent. If the index used by the lender exceeds the rate of growth, the lender cannot take your loan above that level, so the rate is frozen at 14 percent. The following year, the index moves back down below its previous level; however, the terms of your contract specify that you must continue paying the maximum rate of 14 percent, far above the indexed rise, at least until the difference is absorbed.

Or the index may fall, and since the ARM contract might also specify a minimum rate, your rate can never fall below that level. However, not all contracts provide that your rate will be held back until the lender absorbs the difference, even if the index rate rises. When you examine a contract's caps, check carefully to see whether they are calculated on the initial interest rate, or based on the index rate. The two are not always the same. If you don't check them, you might discover later that your cap is higher than you thought.

■ The Teaser Rate

Advertisements for ARM contracts often boast about the extremely low rates being offered. Some institutions euphemistically call this teaser rate the "today rate." What is not advertised, at least not above the small print, is the fact that the low-rate offer ends in a year or two.

Let's say you enter into an ARM contract with payments based on a 7½ percent rate, whereas most ARM contracts are being offered at 8½ percent. Meanwhile, the typical fixed-rate contract is going for 10 percent. You read the ads promising the "lowest rate possible"—the 7½ percent deal—so you take it.

Unfortunately, you may soon discover that the "teaser rate" of 7½ percent is good for only 24 months. After that, the rate automatically goes up to 8½ percent, or more.

Some teasers are even more deceiving. You might be required to make up the difference in interest during the period the teaser rate is in effect. After two years, for example, you might find that one of the following will occur:

- The rate jumps a point higher than the other ARM mortgage

rates, to make up for the lower rate you've been paying. *Read the fine print before you sign anything.* Remember, when the rate goes up, so does your monthly payment. If you sign up for a 7½ percent ARM, which later rises to 10 percent, the difference will be substantial. On a 30-year loan for $100,000, the jump will be about $178 above the original monthly payment.

- An adjustment is made in your balance for interest accrued during the initial 24 months. This means it will take that much longer to pay off your loan, as well as interest on that extra amount. And, of course, with an increase in the balance, more of your current payment will go toward interest.

You might believe you have no choice but to take a teaser rate, because you can't qualify for other terms. Shop around. Avoid deceptive rates and hidden clauses in your contracts. Although lenders should explain the complicated provisions of ARM contracts in detail, they don't always go over it with you. An honest lender will want to ensure that you know exactly what you're getting into. But with the pressure to make money by processing as many loans as time permits, this does not always occur. If you can't get satisfactory answers to your questions about terms of an ARM or any other contract, shop around and place your business somewhere else.

■ Pros and Cons of the Fixed-Rate Mortgage

The traditional form of mortgage, which virtually everyone had until the 1970s, is the fixed-rate mortgage. This mortgage offers an all-important advantage: The amount of the payment will never increase as long as the mortgage remains outstanding, even for 30 years. If you qualify for a fixed-rate mortgage and you can afford the payments, you will enjoy these major advantages:

- You will have the financial security of knowing that your housing costs will be fixed for many years to come. Predictability is a valuable feature.
- You have the flexibility of replacing the mortgage if you later find a cheaper one. You can refinance at any time but will want to do so when rates are lower.
- The real burden of the fixed-rate mortgage actually diminishes over time, due to two things: inflation and your income. Re-

member, your housing costs are fixed. Inflation decreases the fixed payment. (As your income grows, the mortgage payment comes to represent an ever smaller portion of your income.)

The fixed-rate mortgage also comes with some disadvantages:

- Some people simply don't qualify for the favorable rates, so they cannot get a fixed-rate mortgage. This type of loan is available only to those with enough income to qualify.
- You might not be able to come up with enough money for a down payment, which might be higher than for the ARM type of mortgage. You will be asked to put down about 20 percent in most situations. (Some lenders expect a higher down payment for a fixed-rate mortgage, enabling you to qualify for the higher monthly payment.)
- Another disadvantage may be the interest rate itself. Because the rate is fixed, the lender will want to charge an interest rate closer to market rates—higher than what you can get with the ARM. The rate might be one to two points above ARM rates (perhaps even higher, if teaser rates for ARMs are used for comparison).

In addition, the fixed rate becomes a problem when interest rates fall. Once market rates are two points or more below the fixed rate you're paying on your mortgage, it is time to look for a way to refinance. You may be able to cut payments and repayment terms.

■ Negotiating

The terms offered by lenders often can be negotiated, at least to some degree. Whereas the ARM and fixed-rate deals are presented in fixed terms, some things can be altered. You can negotiate:

- The amount of the down payment
- The interest rate
- The number of points or other fees
- The other aspects and conditions, such as rights of conversion from ARM to fixed-rate; payment of processing or application fees; and the speed with which the lender promises to process and approve the loan

Keep in mind that the lender wants to sell you a mortgage, either a fixed-rate or an ARM, that reduces the risks as much as possible for the lender. However, that lender's terms are not carved in stone. Whether there is room for negotiation depends on the current supply and demand—of money and real estate itself. Does the lender need your business, or does the lender have numerous customers clamoring for a limited amount of lendable money? These factors affect how willing the lender will be to negotiate.

You can tell the state of the mortgage market by simply examining the newspaper or radio ads. When lenders are actively seeking borrowers, they "waive" fees, offer no-point or low-point loans, free appraisals, even no-fee loans. When lenders are not seeking more business, you will literally be turned away. If interest rates are so low that the bank cannot turn a profit by selling you a mortgage, or when a particular lender is extended too far into the mortgage market, your business might not be all that appealing.

When business is slow for the lender, you have a much better chance for negotiating successfully. You might be charged fewer points, have some or all fees waived, and even get the advertised interest rate cut. You may be able to offer a smaller down payment (this will apply only if you get a preapproved loan; as a general rule, the down payment is part of the real estate contract). If you have a clean credit record, the lender might be willing to negotiate the down payment and many other contract provisions. If business is slow, try to get a commitment for a fast approval.

Obtaining preapproval is a smart move. It enables you to make an offer on a home without the common financing contingency. Here's how preapproval works:

1. You visit the lender and complete the application. (You will probably have to also prepay a loan application fee.)

2. The lender reviews your credit and verifies your income.

3. When the review is complete, the lender informs you that you qualify for a loan at a specified interest rate. (You might be able to get that rate guaranteed, or locked in, for 60 or 90 days.) The lender also tells you the maximum amount you can borrow based on your current income.

Be a smart mortgage shopper. Check all the conditions and compare. To give yourself greater negotiating room in the real-estate contract, try to get preapproval by a lender. Sellers and agents are very happy to work with a buyer who has been preapproved, because it means there is no problem with financing, which is the most common reason contracts fall apart. Getting preapproval is smart.

■ Tax Laws and Mortgages

Caution: Tax laws are subject to change at any time. Changes may occur when a dispute goes to Tax Court and an important ruling is made. That could affect the way the Internal Revenue Service (I.R.S.) interprets the law. You need to check all tax rules with your tax preparer. The general guidelines below are based on rules in effect as of publication date.

You are allowed to deduct all interest on a mortgage loan used to buy, build, or improve your primary or secondary residences. Therefore, if you live in one house and own a smaller one that you use part of the year, the mortgage interest on loans for both properties qualifies as an itemized deduction. That means that, after you calculate your gross income, you can deduct interest (as well as property taxes and other allowable deductions) instead of using the standard deduction. There is a limit on the mortgage deduction, but it doesn't apply to *most* first-time home buyers: You cannot deduct interest on more than $1 million in mortgages.

Mortgage interest deductions are worth taking because they lower your taxes. This is one of the benefits to owning your own home. An example: A family has an interest deduction of $13,450. Their federal "marginal rate" (the rate charged on their taxable income) is 28 percent, and they pay an additional 6 percent in state taxes. Therefore, they reduce their taxes by 34 percent of the total interest they paid last year:

$13,450 x 34% = $4,573

That savings—$381 per month—is significant. The tax laws are set up to provide a generous subsidy, primarily to encourage people to buy homes. And it works.

Besides the deduction for mortgage interest, you are also allowed to deduct home equity loan interest when that loan is secured by your primary or secondary residence. As far as the $1 million mortgage limit is concerned, the home equity interest deduction can be taken above that limit up to $100,000 if the proceeds are used for home improvements.

■ Variations on Financing

Not every mortgage's terms conform to the most widely used guide-lines of the basic ARM or fixed-rate contract, or are payable over the 15- or 30-year terms. Other rules might also be included in even a standard contract. "Creative financing" became very popular in the late 1970s, when rates were high. The list below includes some of the more popular variations on mortgage financing (most of these terms can be found in current mortgage deals):

Purchase money mortgage. Sometimes a seller, in order to sell a home when the market is slow, will provide the buyer with a mortgage. Called a *purchase money mortgage* or a seller-financed deal, this means that the seller takes a mortgage in exchange for all of the purchase price of the home. The buyer then makes regular mortgage payments to the seller, rather than to an institutional lender, according to the terms of the contract. Although both seller and buyer enjoy some advantages with this arrangement—like the absence of loan fees—such deals can also be risky for both sides. Consult your attorney before signing any contracts with a seller. A contract of this type should specify the interest rate, monthly payment, and due date of the loan.

With a purchase money mortgage, the seller has the right to sell the mortgage to someone else. It often happens that a seller is willing to sell the contract at a discount to an investor, who gets a contract with the full balance due. In exchange, the seller gets a lump sum of cash. For you, the homeowner, your payments simply go to someone else, but the conditions of the deal remain unchanged. The exchange of real estate contracts for discounts can occur frequently with this type of loan.

Graduated-payment mortgage. This is a mortgage designed for those who believe they will be able to afford to pay more at a later date. Monthly payments increase at predetermined intervals, often five to ten years. This means, in some cases, that the loan balance actually *increases* in the early years, because the payments are not enough to cover interest. As a consequence, more interest accrues with each month. This is an expensive condition. You should think carefully before entering into any agreement in which your monthly payments do not decrease the loan balance.

An example: You have a $100,000 loan at 10 percent interest. Over the usual 30-year term, your payments would be $877.58 per month.

One possible variety of graduated-payment mortgage might call for payments of only $725 per month for the first five years. However, that would not be enough to cover the first month's interest of $833, so your balance that month would increase by $108.

After five years, the loan balance would grow to $108,433. Although you will have paid $52,655 by that time, your balance will have increased by $8,433. If you were to pay off this loan in the remaining 25 years, your monthly payment would then have to be $985.

A graduated-payment loan like this is not a good deal. If the payment at least covers interest, it may be worth consideration; but if it doesn't, you only add to the true cost of your home.

Rollover mortgage. This is also called a renegotiable-rate mortgage. It's a financing arrangement in which the interest rate and payment remain constant for a specified period, commonly three to five years. At the end of that time, the terms are renegotiated.

Depending on the volatility of the interest market when you are buying a home, as well as the going rate for mortgage loans, the lender may offer to roll over the loan at a higher or lower rate.

Balloon mortgage. Monthly payments are made at a level rate, usually consisting of interest only. A large payment, called the balloon, is due at the end of the term, often as short as three years from the contract date. The lender will guarantee refinancing in some cases, but the interest rate may not remain the same.

Balloon mortgages are popular for second mortgages offered by some sellers, with a three- or five-year due date, sometimes longer. It is a good idea to make at least a partial payment above the interest only, so that some portion of the principal can be paid down.

Shared-appreciation mortgage. This form is not commonly used today, but it might come back in the future if market conditions change. The mortgage is guaranteed at an interest rate below current market value. In exchange, part of the profits from selling the house will belong to the lender. It may be as high as 30 to 50 percent of the profit. In some contracts, it is payable only upon sale; in others, it becomes due after a specified period of years, whether the house sells or not. If you don't want to sell at that point, you will need to refinance. The payment at the end of the term would be based on current market value by way of appraisal.

When payment is due upon sale, the lender is entitled to 30 percent of the profits on a home purchased for $100,000. But what happens a few years later if you sell the home for $130,000? The lender will receive $9,000 in addition to the proceeds due upon repayment of the loan:

$30,000 x 30% = $9,000

If the lender's portion is due at the end of the term, even if you don't sell, the lender is entitled to part of the appraised market value. In that case, if the home is worth $130,000, you will need to pay the lender a share of the profit.

Shared-equity loan. An investor or family member can help you to buy a home if you cannot afford the down payment, the monthly payment, the property taxes, or other expenses. In return, the investor is entitled to a share of the profits and equity upon sale of the home. You might also be required to pay rent to the investor for his or her portion of the home. Let's say you buy a house for $100,000, with an $80,000 mortgage. An investor puts up $10,000 to match your $10,000 for the down payment. For this, you are required to pay the investor 10 percent per month of the fair-market rent value in the area, representing rent income to the investor—who is entitled to 10 percent on his or her equity. The investor is also entitled to 10 percent of the profit upon sale, and to 10 percent of the equity, even if the house has increased in value.

Wraparound mortgage. This is an all-inclusive mortgage, used more in the West than in the East. It is like a second mortgage, but more complicated. Because questions often arise about who is responsible for taking care of subsequent payments to the lender, both buyer and seller should see an attorney before agreeing to a wraparound mortgage deal.

In this arrangement, you assume an existing low-interest mortgage held by the seller as part of the negotiated real estate contract. The rest of the price is covered by a separate mortgage and a down payment. Both contracts are combined and treated as a single contract, so that the effective interest you pay is a weighted average of the rates on the two mortgages. For example, if you have a $30,000 mortgage at 12 percent, and a $20,000 mortgage at 8 percent, the weighted average applies three-fifths more to the 12 percent mortgage because the loan balance is three-fifths of the total. The weighted average in this case is 10.4 percent: $30,000 at 12% + $20,000 at 8% = $5,200 per year, or 10.4% of the $50,000 total.

The wraparound can also be used when the seller is carrying part of the balance and wants payments to be made on the existing first mortgage, so the seller insists on a wraparound. Under that deal, the buyer makes a total payment to the seller, and the seller then uses part of the payment to cover the original first mortgage.

If the wraparound is used in this way, you could have problems. Although the seller may tell you he or she wants to pay the first mortgage, what assurance do *you* have that the seller will make the payment? A wraparound is tricky and requires cooperation, a written contract, and a thorough understanding of what is being done and what risks are involved. If you enter into a wraparound contract in which someone else makes payments for you, check periodically to make sure those payments *are* being made.

Buy-down mortgage. If you cannot qualify for a mortgage loan at current rates, you might be given one with a lower rate for the first two to five years. The difference is paid by a developer or builder. After the low-rate term, the higher interest rate kicks in. This helps you to qualify for a loan and gets you through the initial few years of financial hardship. In such an arrangement, the developer or builder probably adds the buy-down interest to the price of the home.

Example: A $125,000 home normally would be financed with a 20-percent down payment and a $100,000 loan at 10 percent. Using a buy-down, the buyer is initially charged 8 percent, but the price of the home is raised to $145,000, with 20 percent down ($29,000) and an 80 percent ($116,000) mortgage. The 8-percent rate applies for the first five years; after that, the loan interest increases to 10 percent. The lender gets paid $20,000 ($145,000 - $125,000) in exchange for the buy-down.

Growing-equity mortgage. This is also referred to as a *rapid-payoff mortgage.* Payments increase with each year, and the entire increase goes toward the loan balance. Consequently, the loan is paid off quicker than under a standard contract. It makes sense to use such a device when you expect your annual income to increase and you would like to minimize interest expenses on your mortgage.

The interest rate with this deal is fixed. For example, on a $100,000 mortgage at 10 percent, the normal payment for a 30-year term is $877.58. If the contract calls for annual increases of $75 in the monthly payment, to be added every two years through the eighth year, the payment schedule would be:

Years 1 and 2	$ 877.58
Years 3 and 4	952.58
Years 5 and 6	1,027.58
Years 7 and 8	1,102.58
Years 9 and beyond	1,177.58

The number of years required to pay off the loan is substantially reduced this way. In one variation of this idea, the homeowner makes a monthly payment twice the required amount, and the entire excess goes toward principal. In that case, the entire balance would be paid in full in less than six years.

Reverse-annuity mortgage (RAM). The RAM is granted to people who own their homes free and clear but need a regular monthly income. The homeowner must be over 65 to qualify, and RAMs are offered mainly by insurance companies.

They combine the features of a mortgage with those of an annuity. Payments are made by the company to the homeowner each month. Each payment adds to the balance due on a home mortgage loan, and it grows with interest. The payments, representing an annuity, can go on for the rest of the person's life, or a set number of years may be specified. The insurance company is repaid when the home is sold, when the owner dies, or when the specified period is up (at which time the home usually has to be sold to pay back the RAM). If the homeowner is forced to sell the home and move to pay off the annuity loan, it usually means a loss of all the equity.

A person aged 65 or over with a home worth $100,000 receives approximately $600 per month in the typical RAM. Actual payment levels vary according to the homeowner's age, contractual terms, and rate of interest the insurer uses to calculate its risks. Before entering a RAM contract, you should consult with your attorney.

■ Government Mortgages

Several government agencies insure or guarantee loans to those who meet special requirements.

Veterans Administration (VA) mortgage. The VA grants loans to veterans and their qualified widows. Also called the GI mortgage, this loan is normally guaranteed at a fixed rate lower than the current market rates. VA mortgages require minimal down payments and, at times, no down payments. There are no prepayment penalties (penalties for paying off the loan before its due date), and the mortgage can be assumed by another buyer. Under a VA loan, sellers might have to pay points and some other fees. The term for a VA loan is 30 years.

The loan itself is granted by a savings and loan association or other conventional lender but is guaranteed by the federal government. That is why rates and terms are so favorable. The savings institution assumes virtually no risk.

Not every conventional lender participates in the VA program. The approval period is usually fairly long compared with other lenders, and it must be cleared through the VA. To find out whether you qualify, order the VA's free booklet *Home Loans for Veterans* (Pub. 26-4) by phoning the Veterans Administration at 800-827-1000.

Federal Housing Administration (FHA) mortgage. The FHA works in a way similar to the VA. It insures mortgages granted by commercial lenders for loan applicants who would not otherwise qualify. FHA mortgages feature a down payment as low as 5 percent, closing costs financed rather than paid up front, a 30-year term, no prepayment penalty, and the possibility of a rate below market rates. Before the loan is granted, the home has to pass inspection by an FHA official and has to be appraised by an FHA-approved appraiser.

Approval takes time because of the extra processes the loan goes through. FHA publishes a booklet called *Guide to Single-Family Home Mortgage Insurance.* For information, write to the Federal Housing Administration at 451 7th Street, S.W., Room 9292, Washington, DC, 20410, or telephone 202-708-2700. Some state and local housing agencies have programs similar to the national one sponsored by FHA. Check with local lenders.

Farmers Home Administration (FmHA). The FmHA grants a small number of loans each year, compared with other government agencies. If you live in a rural area, you might qualify. You do not have to be a farmer to get one of these loans. However, your annual income must be below a level established by FmHA.

These loans require little or nothing down, can be paid off over a term as long as 33 years, and are offered at below-market rates. Contact your local FmHA office (in the telephone book under U.S. Government, Department of Agriculture), or write to the Farmers Home Administration, 14th Street and Independence Avenue, S.W., Room 5334-South, Washington, DC, 20250, or telephone 202-720-0099.

■ When Mortgages Are Sold

You should be aware that your mortgage can be sold by your lender any number of times. Lenders often process the paperwork, approve borrowers, advance the money, and then sell the loan to another lender—sometimes even before the first payment is due.

From the lender's point of view, every loan has three different parts: interest, principal, and servicing. The latter refers to collecting your payment, keeping track of escrow funds, paying taxes and insurance when due, calculating payment adjustments in ARM contracts, and mailing out tax notices at the end of the year. Interest and principal are usually transferred to one of the giant government-sponsored mortgage pools, but the servicing stays with the lender, and that's the part that can get sold to someone else.

When your mortgage is sold, you have several rights under a 1990 federal law. First, the old lender is required to send you a "good-bye" letter at least 15 days before your first payment is due to the new lender. Second, you are entitled to a "hello" letter from the new lender within 15 days after your account is transferred. For 60 days after the transfer, you cannot be charged a late fee for making a payment to the previous lender.

You should be highly suspicious if you receive a "hello" letter telling you to begin sending payments to a new lender without having also received a "good-bye" letter from your current lender. Be sure the new lender is for real, or you might discover too late that your money is gone and your mortgage payment is late.

■ Monthly Mortgage Payment Tables

You can estimate your monthly mortgage payments' principal and interest by referring to the following tables. Note that impounds for property taxes, homeowner's insurance, and other insurance payments withheld by the lender are not included.

8% Annual Percent Rate
Monthly Payments (Principal and Interest)

Amount Financed	10 Years	15 Years	20 Years	25 Years	30 Years
$ 25,000	$ 303.32	$ 238.91	$ 209.11	$ 192.95	$ 183.44
35,000	424.65	334.48	292.75	270.14	256.82
45,000	545.97	430.04	376.40	347.32	330.19
50,000	606.64	477.83	418.22	385.91	366.88
60,000	727.97	573.39	501.86	463.09	440.26
70,000	849.29	668.96	585.51	540.27	513.64
80,000	970.62	764.52	669.15	617.45	587.01
90,000	1,091.95	860.09	752.80	694.63	660.39
100,000	1,213.28	955.65	836.44	771.82	733.76
120,000	1,455.94	1,146.78	1,003.72	926.18	880.52
140,000	1,698.58	1,337.92	1,171.02	1,080.54	1,027.28
160,000	1,941.24	1,529.04	1,338.30	1,234.90	1,174.02
180,000	2,183.90	1,720.18	1,505.60	1,389.26	1,320.78
200,000	2,426.56	1,911.30	1,672.88	1,543.64	1,467.52

10% Annual Percent Rate
Monthly Payments (Principal and Interest)

Amount Financed	10 Years	15 Years	20 Years	25 Years	30 Years
$ 25,000	$ 330.38	$ 268.65	$ 241.26	$ 227.18	$ 219.39
35,000	462.53	376.11	337.76	318.05	307.15
45,000	594.68	483.57	434.26	408.92	394.91
50,000	660.75	537.30	482.51	454.35	438.79
60,000	792.90	644.76	579.01	545.22	526.54
70,000	925.06	752.22	675.52	636.09	614.30
80,000	1,057.20	859.68	772.02	726.96	702.06
90,000	1,189.36	967.14	868.52	817.83	789.81
100,000	1,321.51	1,074.61	965.02	908.70	877.57
120,000	1,585.80	1,289.52	1,158.02	1,090.44	1,053.08
140,000	1,850.12	1,504.44	1,351.04	1,272.18	1,228.60
160,000	2,114.40	1,719.36	1,544.04	1,453.92	1,404.12
180,000	2,378.72	1,934.28	1,737.04	1,635.66	1,579.62
200,000	2,643.02	2,149.22	1,930.04	1,817.40	1,755.14

12% Annual Percent Rate
Monthly Payments (Principal and Interest)

Amount Financed	10 Years	15 Years	20 Years	25 Years	30 Years
$ 25,000	$ 358.68	$ 300.05	$ 275.28	$ 263.31	$ 257.16
35,000	502.15	420.06	385.39	368.63	360.02
45,000	645.62	540.08	495.49	473.96	462.88
50,000	717.36	600.09	550.55	526.62	514.31
60,000	860.83	720.11	660.66	631.93	617.17
70,000	1,004.30	840.12	770.77	737.26	720.03
80,000	1,147.77	960.14	880.87	842.58	822.90
90,000	1,291.24	1,080.15	990.98	947.90	925.75
100,000	1,434.71	1,200.17	1,101.09	1,053.23	1,028.62
120,000	1,721.66	1,440.22	1,321.32	1,263.86	1,234.34
140,000	2,008.60	1,680.24	1,541.54	1,474.52	1,440.06
160,000	2,295.54	1,920.28	1,761.74	1,685.16	1,645.80
180,000	2,582.48	2,160.30	1,981.96	1,895.80	1,851.50
200,000	2,869.42	2,400.34	2,202.18	2,106.46	2,057.24

14% Annual Percent Rate
Monthly Payments (Principal and Interest)

Amount Financed	10 Years	15 Years	20 Years	25 Years	30 Years
$ 25,000	$ 388.17	$ 332.94	$ 310.89	$ 300.95	$ 296.22
35,000	543.44	466.11	435.24	421.32	414.71
45,000	698.70	599.29	559.59	541.70	533.20
50,000	776.34	665.88	621.77	601.89	592.44
60,000	931.60	799.05	746.12	722.26	710.93
70,000	1,086.87	932.22	870.47	842.64	829.42
80,000	1,242.14	1,065.40	994.82	963.01	947.90
90,000	1,397.40	1,198.57	1,119.17	1,083.38	1,066.38
100,000	1,552.67	1,331.75	1,243.53	1,203.77	1,184.88
120,000	1,863.20	1,598.10	1,492.24	1,444.52	1,421.86
140,000	2,173.74	1,864.44	1,740.94	1,685.28	1,658.84
160,000	2,484.28	2,130.80	1,989.64	1,926.02	1,895.80
180,000	2,794.80	2,397.14	2,238.34	2,166.76	2,132.76
200,000	3,105.34	2,663.50	2,487.06	2,407.54	2,369.76

13

Mortgage Acceleration Programs

By this point, you certainly understand how expensive it is to buy a home—not because of the asking price, but because interest over the long term adds up to vastly more than the purchase price of the property. At the beginning, most of your payment goes toward interest. If you want to reduce dramatically the actual cost of buying a home, you need to come up with ways to reduce the interest. There are ways to speed up the repayment of a mortgage loan and, in the process, save yourself a lot of money.

Prepayment is called *mortgage acceleration,* and the reasoning behind it is simple: to cut the total cost of your investment by making extra payments. By simply adding more to your monthly payment, when you can afford it, you reduce principal. At the same time, you reduce interest not only for the current period, but for the entire balance of the loan period. Most lender payment slips include space for additional payments to principal. Be sure to let the lender know how you want the payment applied. If the payment slip does not include a space for this, write a note on the payment slip. Also, check in advance with the lender to ensure that the terms of your contract allow you to make prepayments without penalties. Most mortgages allow this up to a limit, but the limit is commonly high enough so that you won't be likely to incur a penalty.

Remember: The earlier in the loan term that you make an accelerated payment, the greater its effect on future interest expense. (For further details, see "How Mortgage Acceleration Works" later in this chapter.)

■ Drawbacks of Acceleration

You can view an acceleration plan as a forced savings account. You will gain a form of savings equal to the amount of interest you save. This gain is represented by the extra payment amount, which is equity in your home.

Remember, though, that investing in equity is not the same as putting cash into a savings account. The money invested in the home is *not* available to you like the money in the bank down the street. You cannot simply withdraw your extra principal payments. You would have to refinance or take out a second mortgage to get your equity out, which is an expensive process involving closing costs that include a credit check, an appraisal, points, and processing fees—not to mention the time it takes to cash in equity. For your own peace of mind, be sure that the money you put into any mortgage acceleration plan is money you can afford to be without for several years.

Another drawback to mortgage acceleration is that it might not fit well into your household budget. Before starting a savings plan that ties up your money, make sure you have a savings account large enough to meet any emergencies. Many financial experts suggest that a family should have savings equal to three to six months' income, just as an emergency fund. Decide for yourself how much you need, based on your ideas of risk and the need for a financial safety net.

If your car breaks down, how will you pay for repairs? If your children have an unexpected medical or dental expense not covered by insurance, how will you pay for it? Of even greater concern is the possibility that you or your spouse will lose your job tomorrow or next week. How will you support yourself while you look for another job? Emergencies are rarely predictable, thus the need for some careful planning.

Some families depend on lines of credit through credit cards rather than setting up a savings account. If you have adequate credit and a secure job, this is one alternative and, for many people, a comfortable one. It's a question of risk: How much risk can you afford, and how much risk are you willing to assume?

■ Shorter Mortgage Terms: One Possible Answer

One way to accelerate your mortgage is by setting up a shorter mortgage term at the time you negotiate the loan. Shorter-term mortgages work just like the 30-year kind, but the lender may offer a lower interest rate. Generally, rates for 15-year mortgages may run between one-quarter and three-quarters of a percentage point lower than the 30-year mortgage. By speeding up the repayment date, you will save tens of thousands of dollars in interest and repay the loan in half the time. The difference in repayment terms between a 30- and a 15-year mortgage is shown in Figure 13.1, based on a 10 percent loan.

Table 13.1 The Real Cost of a Mortgage

Monthly payments for a $100,000 fixed-rate mortgage. (Shorter-term loans usually have slightly lower interest rate charges.)

Type of Mortgage	Interest	Months Paid	Monthly Payment	Total Finance Charges
10-year	10.25%	120	$1,335	$ 60,247
15-year	10.25	180	1,090	96,191
20-year	10.25	240	982	135,594
30-year	10.5	360	915	229,306

Prepayments on a $100,000, 30-year fixed-rate mortgage

$100 per month	10.5%	228	$1,015	$130,924
50 per month	10.5	273	965	162,998
25 per month	10.5	307	940	188,575

Of course, each monthly payment on a shorter-term mortgage is noticeably higher. The shorter the loan term, the higher the payments. But the difference may not be as much as you'd think.

That difference, no matter how small, makes it harder to qualify for a shorter-term loan. Most lenders don't like to see more than a certain

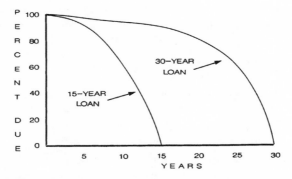

Figure 13.1 Rates of Decline in a Loan's Balance

percent of your gross monthly income spent on monthly mortgage payments. If the percentage of your income required to make a loan payment is too high, your application will be rejected. The alternative to a shorter-term loan: Sign up for the 30-year loan but make voluntary payments at the rate required to pay it off over 15 years.

■ Other Mortgage Acceleration Options

Some types of mortgages can help you to accelerate payments and reduce interest costs. These include:

Biweekly mortgages. In a biweekly arrangement, you pay one-half of the monthly mortgage every two weeks, rather than paying the entire amount once per month. Because there are 52 weeks in the year, you end up making 26 half-monthly payments, or 13 full payments per year. This additional annual payment goes toward accelerating the loan. For example, if your $100,000, 30-year mortgage were paid on a biweekly schedule rather than on a monthly schedule, and the interest rate were 10.5 percent, you would save nearly $86,000 in interest over the life of the loan.

Lenders may offer to administer your payments on a biweekly schedule. This idea is frequently offered by financing firms or financial planners for fees ranging between $300 and $500 to set up the plan. The programs are sold as forms of "free" insurance. For example, a planning firm might advertise that they will provide you with free insurance *and* cut the cost of your mortgage. By saving an average of $2,800 per year by cutting your mortgage costs, you can afford to pay $2,200 per year for life insurance. Because you are cutting interest, the insurance is "free" and, above and beyond that, you still come out ahead by $600 per year.

However, you can keep all of the savings for yourself by instituting the equivalent of a biweekly plan on your own, without paying any set-up fees and without buying insurance you don't really need. Here's how: Simply divide your monthly mortgage payment by 12, and then add that amount to each monthly payment. If you are paying $914.74 per month on a $100,000, 30-year mortgage, just add one-twelfth of that amount, or $76.23, to the payment. Then make equal monthly payments of $990.97. This achieves precisely the same effect as a biweekly mortgage, without the cost. And you keep *all* of the savings.

Convertible mortgages. Often called a reduction option, or rate-improvement loan, the convertible mortgage provides you with a one-time opportunity to lock in a lower interest rate, usually at any point between the second and fifth years of your loan term. This helps you avoid having to refinance every time rates fall. Lenders offer this privilege for a relatively small conversion fee as a means of ensuring that the fixed rate can be adjusted if, in the future, rates drop substantially.

The terms of your contract may provide that you can exercise the right only if the lender's rates fall by a specified amount, such as two points below the original rate on your loan. If you do lock in the new rate, your monthly payments will drop for the remainder of the loan term. In most cases, all you need to do to lock in a lower rate is contact the lender in writing and pay a conversion fee, usually between $250 and $500.

■ Prepayment Policies

Lenders vary in their prepayment policies. Some assess no penalties whatsoever, whereas others impose limits, usually expressed as a percentage of the loan's balance (or a percentage of the original loan amount) that can be prepaid each year. If you exceed those limits, you will be charged a prepayment penalty. In some states and with certain types of loans, terms of prepayment are a matter of law. For example, in Massachusetts lenders are restricted as to when and how they can assess penalties; and in California institutions cannot assess a prepayment penalty if a borrower refinances with the same institution.

Every mortgage contract should clearly spell out the prevailing prepayment rules: the amount the institution allows you to prepay each year without penalty, the extent of the penalty if imposed, and the timing of prepayments. Be certain you understand the language and ramifications of any prepayment clauses before agreeing to the terms of the mortgage.

The most common provision permits you to prepay up to one-fifth of the original loan balance each year without penalty. Anything above that level is penalized, assuming such penalties are not forbidden by state law.

How large are the potential savings for prepayment? Consider the cost of borrowing money over a long period of time. With a 30-year mortgage at the rate of 10 percent interest, payments add up as follows:

Loan Amount	Total Payments	Total Interest
$ 50,000	$157,963	$107,963
60,000	189,555	129,555
70,000	221,148	151,148
80,000	252,740	172,740
90,000	284,333	194,333
100,000	315,926	215,926
125,000	394,907	269,907
150,000	473,889	323,889
175,000	552,870	377,870
200,000	631,852	431,852

Over 30 years, your monthly payments would total more than three times the original loan amount. That's why it is worthwhile to consider mortgage acceleration as an important part of your financial planning.

■ How Mortgage Acceleration Works

Mortgage acceleration is nothing more than paying a greater monthly payment than required by contract. For many families, that just isn't possible. Without a cash reserve or extra money in the budget, mortgage acceleration might have to wait. However, if you can afford extra payments—even a very small amount—you will get a worthwhile return. Here are some important facts to keep in mind if you're thinking about mortgage acceleration:

- The percentage of principal paid off in a 30-year loan by the 25th year is about one-half of the original amount borrowed. The remaining half of principal is paid off during the last five years. The exact percentage varies according to the interest rate:

Interest Rate	Paid off by 25th Year
7%	66.4%
8	63.8
9	61.2
10	58.7
11	56.2
12	53.8
13	51.4
14	49.1
15	46.9

- An extra month's payment at the beginning of a 30-year mortgage term will reduce the time needed for repayment by one year. Suppose you have a $100,000 30-year mortgage at 10 percent, with a monthly payment of $877.58. If you pay $1,755.16 in the first month (doubling the required payment just once), your loan will be paid off in about 29 years.
- A loan period can be cut in half if each month's principal payment is doubled. For example, a 30-year, $100,000 loan at 10 percent would be paid off in 15 years and one month. Because you would increase each month's payment by an amount that matches the (increasing) amount of principal due as interest diminishes, payments would start at $921.81, growing to $1,779 by the end of the 15th year.
- The same loan will be paid off in 15 years if you make equal monthly payments of $1,074.61.
- The same loan can be paid in full in five years and three months if each month's payment is doubled from $1,074.61 to $2,149.22.

These statistics certainly point out how acceleration reduces the total cost of buying a home. However, you have to be able to afford the extra payments.

By doubling your payments, the home would cost a total of $128,953, of which $28,953 is interest. With the normal 30-year payment schedule, you would pay a total of $315,925, of which $215,925 is interest. In other words, by doubling the monthly payment, you would save an impressive $186,972 in interest and cut 25 years off the time required for repaying your mortgage.

The forms of mortgage acceleration that are the most dramatic are also the least affordable for most of us. However, you can devise a tailored mortgage acceleration plan to fit your own circumstances. You can repay your mortgage at your own rate and discretion, suspending, stopping, or increasing the method at will—as long as the terms of your loan provide you with the right to prepay without penalty. You do not need permission to prepay; simply mail in more money than required and make sure you instruct the lender to apply it to principal.

A small amount added to the payment has a big effect over the term of a loan. Using the example of a 30-year, $100,000 mortgage at 10 percent interest, Table 13.2 shows payments without any acceleration; Table 13.3 illustrates the effect of an extra payment to principal of $100 per month.

Table 13.2 Full Amortization

Month	Payment	Interest	Principal	Balance
				$100,000.00
1	$877.57	$833.33	$44.24	99,955.76
2	877.57	832.96	44.61	99,911.15
3	877.57	832.59	44.98	99,866.17
4	877.57	832.22	45.35	99,820.82
5	877.57	831.84	45.73	99,775.09
6	877.57	831.46	46.11	99,728.98
7	877.57	831.07	46.50	99,682.48
8	877.57	830.69	46.88	99,635.60
9	877.57	830.30	47.27	99,588.33
10	877.57	829.90	47.67	99,540.66
11	877.57	829.50	48.07	99,492.59
12	877.57	829.10	48.47	99,444.12
Total	$10,530.84	$9,974.96	$555.88	—

Table 13.3 Amortization with $100 Extra

Month	Payment	Interest	Principal	Balance
				$100,000.00
1	$977.57	$833.33	$144.24	99,855.76
2	977.57	832.13	145.44	99,710.32
3	977.57	830.92	146.65	99,563.67
4	977.57	829.70	147.87	99,415.80
5	977.57	828.46	149.11	99,266.69
6	977.57	827.22	150.35	99,116.34
7	977.57	825.97	151.60	98,964.74
8	977.57	824.70	152.87	98,811.87
9	977.57	823.43	154.14	98,657.73
10	977.57	822.15	155.42	98,502.31
11	977.57	820.85	156.72	98,345.59
12	977.57	819.55	158.02	98,187.57
Total	$11,730.84	$9,918.41	$1,182.43	—

As the tables demonstrate, total interest is reduced by $57 and the total balance due by $1,257 (interest saved in the year, plus $100 per month). Interest will be lower each and every month from that point forward because the loan's balance is lower, meaning that the reduction of a balance in the first year has a compounding effect over the rest of the mortgage term.

When an acceleration program is put into effect, the extra money paid against the mortgage balance is not spent. It's saved, and you will pay off the mortgage more rapidly as a result.

If your mortgage rate is 10 percent, acceleration is the same as getting 10 percent on another investment. Acceleration is often questioned on this basis. Some people argue that you should pay your mortgage normally and invest the rest of your money in other ways. However, that is good advice only if the interest rate on the mortgage is lower than the investment rate elsewhere. Historically, this kind of investment has been difficult to find—especially an investment that is as safe and secure as your own home.

By insuring your home's value (through homeowner's insurance), you maintain its investment value. To a large extent, future value is within *your* control. Few other investments contain such features.

Therefore, when evaluating acceleration as an investment for your savings, be sure that the alternatives are comparable. There is no point in comparing the rate of return on an extremely safe, insured investment to one that offers no guarantees, where you could lose money.

■ ARMs and Mortgage Acceleration

So far, we've only discussed mortgage acceleration using a 30-year fixed-rate mortgage as an example. However, acceleration programs also work with ARM contracts, often to a greater degree.

For example, let's say you have an ARM that starts out at 9 percent. Over time, the rate is increased between 10 and 14 percent. The higher the rate, the greater the reason to make accelerated payments. Remember, the rate you're paying on the mortgage is the equivalent of a savings rate for every dollar you accelerate. Given that argument, you should accelerate more as the interest rate increases. However, you also have to remember that the required payment will be higher whether you accelerate or not. The difference between payments at 9 percent and at 14 percent, on a $100,000, 30-year mortgage, is $380 per month.

Here's an alternate argument: It makes as much sense to accelerate at the lower rate for two reasons. With payments lower than they might be in the future, you can afford to put more extra cash into additional payments. In addition, acceleration reduces future interest when rates do rise because the principal balance will be reduced. As a result, the higher rates of interest will translate to less overall interest if you accelerate early on.

With an ARM, you are contractually required to make the payment needed to amortize the loan with the applicable rate. Since an accelerated loan will require lower monthly payments in the future, the cumulative effects of early acceleration will be realized later on, when the lender increases your interest rate.

Mortgage acceleration can be a valuable planning tool to offset the effects of changing interest rates under an ARM contract. However, you should always be careful to compare current investment rates of relatively safe programs before committing to mortgage acceleration. Be sure to make your comparison on an after-tax basis. Just as mortgage interest is deductible, income from other investments is also usually taxable. In some markets, you can do better than you would with acceleration. Check the whole market before you decide which way to go.

Insurance

14

The Homeowner's Policy

Most people think of fire when they hear the term homeowner's insurance. Certainly, fires are the most expensive and common source of homeowner's insurance claims. Losses from fires and their consequences (smoke and water damage) account for more than $3 billion every year in the United States, just in single- and double-unit housing. According to the National Fire Protection Association, about 350,000 fires occur in residences every year. Given the volume of fires and the amount of damage caused, it's important to make sure you have enough coverage to protect your home and your belongings.

Unfortunately, many Americans do not know what their homes or the personal property inside a home are worth. It was once safe to believe that personal property should be estimated at between one-fourth and one-half of a home's value. Today, personal property values have grown relative to the value of homes because people continue to buy expensive items, like computers and electronic equipment. Current homeowners probably need to insure personal property up to 100 percent of their home's replacement value; some insurance agents recommend going to that level automatically.

■ Required Coverage

A homeowner's policy covers more than just fires. It is divided into two parts: liability and casualty protection. Liability protects you in the event someone is injured while on your property. For example, if a visitor trips over a garden hose, or slips on a wet sidewalk, or is injured while swimming in your pool, you could be sued. In that case, your liability insurance would pay the claim.

Casualty insurance covers losses to your property. These losses may be natural or manmade, including fires, weather damage, vandalism, theft, and robbery. Lenders require you to carry homeowner's insurance as long as there is any balance still due on your mortgage. If you did not have homeowner's insurance and you suffered a loss, the lender would be in a difficult position, and perhaps would be unable to recover the value of the mortgage. Once a house is paid off, you don't have to carry insurance, but considering the relatively low cost, it makes sense to continue to protect your property. A fire or other disaster could wipe out all of your equity in a matter of moments.

Some ill-advised homeowners allow their insurance policies to lapse after their mortgages are repaid in full; 3 percent of *all* American homeowners do not carry insurance.

The cost of replacing your uninsured home and everything in it is not a pleasant prospect. A good rule of thumb concerning fire insurance, like all types of insurance, is this: If you cannot afford the economic loss that would result from a disaster, then you need to protect yourself against that consequence by buying insurance.

Even if you maintain your insurance policy, you still face the risk of underinsuring your property. You need to review your policy now and then—at least once per year—and update it. Or you may also purchase insurance that provides for full replacement of your home and all your belongings, even if market values have increased substantially. The key element in such a policy is "guaranteed replacement." That means that your home will be replaced for whatever it costs, and to the same standards as it currently exists.

■ Updating Your Policy

Unfortunately, many homeowners tend to ignore their insurance policies. Don't be one of them. Even though reviewing your policy is not the most exciting way to spend a Saturday night, it is important. Because insurance is complicated, frustrating, and technical, it's easy to put off the review.

The frequency of updating your policy depends on a variety of conditions, including:

- Whether market values and construction costs in your area are increasing.
- Whether the value of your personal property—everything inside the home—has grown recently.
- Whether you have recently completed an expensive home improvement project, or you are beginning such a project.

Some insurance policies automatically increase the amount of coverage each year. The increase is often based on changes in the Consumer Price Index (CPI) or on a stated version of the CPI, depending on which insurance carrier wrote your policy. Of course, you will have to pay a higher premium for this coverage.

You should also be aware that you might need additional, special coverage for some items, since the standard policy will not cover their loss. For example, most policies won't cover business assets kept in your home, and they also contain fairly low limits for art collections, jewelry and furs, and collectibles. Therefore, if you operate a business from your home or you collect anything of exceptional value, you will need to talk to your insurance agent and ask for a rider (extra coverage for those assets). Also, make yourself aware of any additional exceptions listed in your policy.

■ How to Buy Insurance

The problem of underinsurance may occur when you first buy your home. In the midst of all the red tape, the deadlines of closing, and the confusion about inspections, filing fees, contingencies, and handing over a huge sum of money, insurance matters may be left unattended. It often happens that the real estate agent, lender, or escrow agent automatically places the insurance policy with an insurance agent he or she uses time and again. The policy may be written by someone who never even sees your home but estimates the premium based on your address and the amount of coverage based on the purchase price. The amount of coverage should be based on what would be required to replace the home. In any event, your lender will require adequate coverage to protect its position, recognizing that you don't need coverage for land. Personal property is assigned a value based on the home's value, a reasonable *average* but not necessarily applicable to you.

The first year's premium is listed as one of many closing costs, and the monthly payment for the following year is included in impounds (amounts added to your monthly mortgage payment). With this procedure, you never even have to meet the insurance agent. You receive a copy of the policy along with a stack of other closing documents. For a large segment of home buyers, this is a typical scenario.

This is also *not* the way to buy homeowner's insurance. It initiates a casual attitude toward your risk, the costs involved, and degree of protection. Instead of having insurance provided in this way, insist on choosing your own policy. Interview insurance agents and find one who is willing to sit down with you, explain the options available, ask you what kind of coverage you want and need, and recommend the best alternatives. Ask the agent to explain the various riders you can attach to a policy. For example, if you run a small part-time business from your home, how can you get insurance for your computer? If you have a stamp or coin collection or some valuable art, can the agent provide extra insurance for those items? Also, find out about inflation adjustments in coverage, and study the cost and benefit trade-offs in setting different levels of deductibles (the portion you will have to pay for any claims). Some insurance companies offer discounts if you place more than one policy with them. As a result, it might make sense to place your homeowner's, auto, and life insurance through the same agent, as well as any other policies you carry. Many companies are able to combine dissimilar policy coverages under one "umbrella" policy.

When buying your first homeowner's insurance policy, don't skimp on coverage to save a few dollars. It's a big mistake to pay a lower annual premium and, in the process, give up insurance coverage you actually need to have. Cheaper policies may have more exclusions or greatly limit the amount of a claim you will be allowed to collect in the event of a loss. By saving some money, you could be living with more risk than you can afford. Keep in mind, though, that not all insurance companies offer comparable coverage for the same rates. Prices of insurance vary not only from state to state but also from neighborhood to neighborhood. The rate varies based on whether your house is constructed of brick or wood; the distance to the closest fire station and fire hydrant; and the number of fires in that area over the past year or two.

Price, however, is an important buying criterion. Rates for the same coverage in the same area can vary by 50 to 100 percent, depending on the company you pick. You have to do some comparison shopping. In order to make an informed decision, be sure that you *are* comparing the same level and degree of coverage; otherwise, you will not be making a valid comparison. First, decide what losses you need to cover. Here, an informative and patient insurance agent is a valuable source of help. Next, ask for quotes from at least three companies. Remember, homeowner's insurance is a fairly standardized product, with only a few variations available. Base your decision on price versus claims service, and individual agent service.

Claims service will ultimately be important if you ever have to put in a claim. Disturbing as it might seem, many companies have a dismal record of helping their customers after they suffer a loss. About one of every four policyholders who file claims has at least one complaint about the insurance company's service or about the way their claim was handled, according to a *Consumer Reports* survey of 47,000 readers who filed claims between January 1989 and spring 1992. Although complaints were widespread, most consumers were reimbursed for their losses in a reasonable amount of time. The average insurance company paid 81 percent of claims within 30 days of filing.

For problems with service or response, or questions about an insurance agent's licensing, contact your state insurance department. Or you can call the Insurance Information Institute at 800-942-4242 for more information about homeowner's insurance.

▪ How Much Is Enough?

In order to know how much insurance you need, you first have to determine how much your home and personal possessions are worth. Remember: These values are *not* permanent. They will change frequently as you acquire more, and as the value of property grows. There are several ways to judge ever-changing values.

On your home:

- Hire an appraiser. Costs vary, since appraisals are not regulated in most states. A Member, Appraisal Institute (MAI)—an individual who has undergone an extensive series of tests and has been granted an appraisal license—is considered the highest authority in the field. An MAI appraisal will probably be more expensive than one by a non-MAI, an unlicensed appraiser, or a lender.

- Ask a real estate agent's opinion. This is not only less expensive than hiring an appraiser; it's usually faster, too. An agent looks at a home with the market in mind, and can usually give you a good rough idea of its market value. It is not reasonable, however, to expect an agent to come to your home and give you a free appraisal if you don't intend to sell.

- Check the market. Besides asking agents their opinions, look in the paper. What's for sale in your area, and what are the asking prices? If neighbors have comparable homes for sale, what are they asking? Talk to a lender or real estate agent and ask about average sales prices for homes like yours over the past year.

- Estimate the replacement cost of your home. Replacement values vary from one area to another, and are usually expressed in a dollar value per square foot. On this basis, any building contractor can tell you the replacement value in your area. Multiply that dollar value by the square feet in your home. That is the replacement value. Don't confuse *replacement value* with *market value*. The replacement value refers only to the amount required to rebuild a home. Market value is the current value including the land.

For your possessions:

- Write up a detailed inventory of all your belongings. Keep the list in a safe place such as a safe-deposit box or your insurance agent's office. Do *not* keep the list in the home, as it would be lost with everything else in the event of a fire. Accompany your list with a video tape of every room, being sure to get on film all of the property you own. If you later need to put in a claim, the tape not only verifies what you own, it will also help you to recall all of your possessions so you can file a complete claim. The total cost of all your furniture, clothing, electronic equipment, and appliances is the least amount of insurance you should carry. Don't automatically accept an insurance company's estimate based on the value of the home.

- Keep receipts for major purchases in the same place as your inventory and video of your possessions. Include appliances, electronic gear, exercise equipment, computer hardware and software, and anything else you own that costs a lot.

- Write up a separate inventory of all jewelry, furs, collections, and business equipment. Be prepared to verify the value of these items with purchase receipts or independent professional appraisals; keep these in a safe place with photographs of the items, and don't forget to buy extra insurance to cover their value.

Even with these steps, be sure you know the dollar limits on special items as well as the overall limits, if they apply, on replacing normal items like furniture and clothing. You may need to buy a *floater,* either a separate policy or an endorsement to the homeowner's policy, to cover any value above standard limits. This applies to items such as jewelry. In a floater, the property covered has to be "scheduled," meaning listed and described specifically by quantity, quality, style, manufacturer, and value. You may also need an appraisal simply to establish the value, even if you have receipts.

Floaters may cost anything from a few dollars per year per $100 of coverage up to a higher level. Another factor influencing the cost of such insurance will be the crime rate in your area. The higher the risk of loss, the more you will have to pay for any extra coverage.

■ Cutting Costs

You can reduce the cost of insurance in several ways:

- Accept a higher deductible. This means that in the event of a loss, you will have to pay more, but premiums will be considerably less. For example, by increasing your casualty deductible from $100 to $250, you will save substantially on the cost of the policy.
- Install security devices, such as deadbolt locks and an electronic security system, in your home. Besides giving you an extra measure of security, these will also reduce your cost of insurance.
- Install fire and smoke alarms. These are mandatory in newly built apartments and houses. Many insurers offer discounts for installing these devices.
- Comparison shop. Compare rates for homeowner's insurance

among three or more carriers, but be sure you're not comparing apples to oranges. Write down the types and limits of coverage and the deductible levels. Don't look only at the cost of premiums.

- Consider buying one combined policy, or at least placing different types of insurance with one carrier. Some companies will discount all of your coverage in exchange for getting all of your business. Insurers add a "load" to every policy they write to cover general and administrative costs and the selling agent's commission. By combining several policies, you may be able to save 10 to 15 percent overall on premium costs. Be wary of large discounts offered by insurers, however. They might inflate their starting rate just to advertise their big discounts. Compare. Remember, you're buying insurance, not furniture. You have to be careful to look at comparable rates for comparable coverage.
- Compare various terms and definitions used by insurance companies. Figure out the best way to protect yourself against losses.

Although not a way to reduce the cost of a policy, buying guaranteed replacement insurance will save you money in the event of a loss. It's good coverage for your home and for your personal property. Watch out, however, for any overall ceilings placed on what a policy will pay. For example, your policy might limit a reimbursement to an amount equal to 400 percent of "actual cash value." If a possession was bought for $2,000, you won't necessarily get back enough to replace its current value. "Actual cash value" (replacement value minus depreciation) is calculated by the insurance company. If they calculate the current actual cash value of that asset to be $300, the maximum reimbursement you will get—400 percent—will be $1,200. This coverage, although not ideal, is still better than one offering only actual cash value. In the above example, actual-cash-value coverage would provide only a $300 reimbursement for the depreciated asset. Such coverage does not keep up with inflation. Rather, it calculates what your possessions are worth today based on how old they are.

15

Liability Protection

One of the greatest risks you face when becoming a homeowner is exposure to liability. If someone is injured while on your property, you can be sued for damages.

You can be held responsible not only for the immediate damages, such as medical bills the injured person incurs, but also for the time that person loses from work (which can be substantial) and "pain and suffering" as well.

Some of the types of injuries covered under "liability" arise from circumstances beyond your control. For example, if a limb falls from your tree and injures a passing pedestrian, you can be sued—just because the tree is on your property. The fact that you did not directly cause the injury does not matter. The complaint could charge that you should have known the limb was weak and could fall, or that you knew and neglected to saw it off. You might be able to successfully defend against such claims, but the argument is frequently made in liability cases that homeowners could have prevented an accident in some way.

Here's another example: A neighbor's child is teasing your dog through the fence. The dog bites the child. Common sense says that the child caused the injury, but in the world of liability you are responsible for the dog's behavior. Medical costs, pain and suffering, and other injuries could be assessed because you didn't supervise the dog, or because you didn't build a better fence to prevent the dog from biting someone.

A judge or jury could rule that an injured person shares part of the blame. This is referred to as "comparative" negligence. The award will be based on the determined level of fault. For example, let's say your ladder has a weak rung that you plan to have fixed, but a neighbor borrows your ladder without your permission and climbs onto your roof to retrieve a ball. The weak rung snaps and he falls, breaking his leg. Who is at fault? The neighbor may blame you for leaving the dangerously defective ladder where he could find it; you may claim he had no business using your ladder or going up on your roof. The courts might recognize that both sides share some responsibility for the accident.

Another form of partial fault is called "contributory" negligence. This occurs when someone sues for damages and, although you were at fault, the injured party was even more at fault. In other words, your contributory negligence was minor compared with the other person's negligence. Going back to the example of the neighbor and the ladder, suppose your neighbor had been drinking heavily, or that he went into your closed workshop to find the ladder. Given these additional circumstances, the balance of fault shifts more toward the neighbor.

Cases of liability are usually handled entirely by your insurance company. Although the company's attorney might ask for a statement from you, chances are you won't have to actually go to court. If the company does have a liability, they will usually settle up with the neighbor without your having to spend hours in a courtroom.

■ What Is Covered?

Personal liability is a claim for damages resulting from your negligence. If such a claim is filed and you have no insurance, your home— as well as every other asset you own—could be taken away to satisfy a judgment against you in court. Even your future earnings could be attached and assigned to an injured person. In other words, such a lawsuit could wipe you out financially.

Homeowner's policies in past years have offered a minimum of $25,000 coverage for liability for bodily injury and property damage. However, in today's litigious environment, many insurance companies offer minimums of $100,000 or more. For an extra $10 in annual premiums, you can get about $300,000 of liability coverage, a small extra cost well worth paying.

A homeowner's policy should cover these potential claims:

Medical payments. Medical bills add up quickly, even for small injuries. Some injuries require repeated visits to physicians, physical therapy, or a stay in the hospital, sometimes for many days or even weeks. Moreover, medical benefits may be paid for an injured person, regardless of who is really at fault. Someone who is injured on your property through his or her own negligence might still be able to file a claim against your insurance company for medical payments.

Injuries and property damage. Someone can file a claim against you after suffering a loss while on your property, or because an incident took place on your land. This can be done regardless of whether you were at fault, the victim's own actions caused the injury, or even if it was an act of God. For example, if a limb falls from a tree and hits your neighbor, or your 12-year-old child throws a rock and injures someone, or your pesticide is blown over to your neighbor's property, killing his outdoor ornamental goldfish or a prized shrub, these are covered under your liability protection.

Loss of earnings. If someone is injured on your property and as a result cannot work, your policy covers his or her lost wages. Depending on the nature of the injury and the amount of work time lost, this can add up to a significant sum of money.

Pain and suffering. This is the most difficult loss to assign value to, but juries do it all the time. Their judgment could result in an extremely high cash award for an injured person.

■ What Isn't Covered

Some forms of personal injury are *not* covered under your homeowner's policy. These include:

Work-related losses. Most policies specifically exclude injuries or damages incurred for work-related activities. As a result, if you have a business at home and clients or associates regularly come to your home, you will need to buy extra liability insurance to cover you. For example, let's say you run a bookkeeping business from your home, and your clients drop by to pick up or deliver their books each month. On one visit, a client trips over your sprinkler and breaks her ankle; she files a claim against you. Because her visit was work-related, a standard liability policy will *not* cover the loss. For a small annual premium, you can obtain additional coverage or get a separate business policy.

Another example: You are having a garage sale and someone stops to look at what you're selling. While there, he trips on your steps and falls, breaking his arm. You might or might not be covered. If you hold garage sales only once per year, it's not a business; if you hold them every weekend, it probably qualifies as a business and you will not be protected against liability under your standard homeowner's policy.

Another problem might arise if you hire a contractor for an improvement or renovation. Make sure the contractor has liability protection *and* worker's compensation for employees, as well as performance bonds for subcontractors. Otherwise, you—as the property owner—could be exposed to liability for any injuries or damages occurring while the contractor is on your property.

Malpractice. Liability policies for professionals who work out of their homes do *not* include malpractice insurance protection. That coverage must be obtained through a separate policy.

Working children. Even though liability insurance covers you and your family, you could have a potential problem if your child does yard work or odd jobs for other people. For example, liabilities occurring while your child is on a newspaper route might be excluded. If your child bikes through a flower bed or knocks someone over with his bicycle, you might not be covered for those events if the child is earning money at the time.

Extra coverage is cheap. If your child has a job, a small annual premium will protect you from potentially large liability claims.

Second homes or vacation property. Your homeowner's policy will not cover liabilities related to investment properties or a second home. You need separate coverage for each property.

Automobiles and other vehicles. Your homeowner's policy does not include accidents in your car, boat, or plane. You need separate insurance for all vehicles.

Domestic employees. If you hire a gardener, housekeeper, or regular baby-sitter, you probably need extra liability coverage. You will also need to buy workers compensation insurance and may be subject to federal and state withholding laws for other forms of required insurance. Even if those requirements don't apply in your situation, buying extra liability insurance is a smart idea.

Intentional damage. You are never covered for any damages you do to your own property or for injuries you intentionally inflict on others.

In summary, considering the infinite variety of situations in which you can be held liable for claims, and considering the relatively low cost of liability insurance, it's better to have too much coverage than too little. You should definitely carry a minimum of $300,000 of liability insurance; you may consider carrying more. Check with your insurance agent to see how much it will cost.

Some people take out an "umbrella" policy, which offers protection for many more risks than the standard injuries that can occur around the house. This extra coverage is above and beyond the normal homeowner's policy insurance. For a fairly small annual premium, you can be protected against a wide array of potential problems, including claims arising from business activity, libel and slander, and other losses most people never worry about. This type of protection is advisable if you have a higher-than-average net worth, if you work from the home, or if your home is worth much more than the average home in your area.

16

Casualty Protection

According to the National Fire Protection Association, a fire breaks out in a home in the United States every 90 seconds. More than 28,000 people are injured and approximately 4,700 are killed each year in such fires, and property losses amount to more than $3 billion. Fire is the most common casualty covered by homeowner's insurance.

Casualties are damages, losses, or accidents to your home and belongings. Whereas liability insurance protects you against losses and injuries to others, casualty insurance is designed to reimburse you for damages to your home and furnishings.

Fire insurance was the first type of casualty protection. Compared with fires, other casualties account for only a minor portion of total insurance claims; hence, homeowner's insurance is often referred to as "fire insurance." You pay substantial premiums primarily because residential fires are so costly.

About 15 percent of fires in homes result from arson or are of "suspicious" origin. The rest are accidental, caused by children playing with matches, smokers falling asleep in bed with lighted cigarettes, kitchen flare-ups, or electrical wiring defects, for example. Considering the range of things that can go wrong and start a fire in your home, the need for insurance coverage should be obvious.

■ What Is Covered?

Eleven kinds of casualties are covered in every homeowner's policy, and are referred to as the "11 common perils." You are covered for damages caused by:

1. Fire or lightning

2. Loss of property removed from the premises because of fire or other perils

3. Windstorm or hail

4. Explosion

5. Riots and other civil commotion

6. Aircraft

7. Vehicles

8. Smoke

9. Vandalism and malicious mischief

10. Theft

11. Breakage of glass that constitutes a part of the building

A policy covering only these 11 perils is called an HO-1 policy (HO stands for homeowner). Seven additional forms of casualty are included in some expanded policy forms. These are losses from:

12. Falling objects

13. Weight of ice or snow

14. Collapse of a building or any part thereof

15. Sudden and accidental tearing apart, cracking, burning, or bulging of a steam or hot water heating system or of appliances for heating water

16. Accidental discharge, leakage, or overflow of water or steam from within a plumbing, heating, or air-conditioning system or a domestic appliance

17. Freezing of plumbing, heating, and air-conditioning systems and domestic appliances

18. Sudden and accidental injury from electrical currents generated by appliances, devices, fixtures, and wiring (TV and radio tubes are not included)

A policy covering all 18 perils is called an HO-2 or HO-4 policy (see the next section for more explanation of different types of policies).

Even more protection can be obtained in an "all risks" policy, which extends coverage to "all perils except flood, earthquake, war, nuclear accident, and others specified in your policy." This version is called an HO-3 or HO-5 policy.

Like liability insurance, casualty protection is relatively inexpensive but varies depending on the size, location, and construction of your home. However, the damages inflicted by common perils can be extremely costly to repair. A good rule of thumb you should follow is: The more casualty insurance you carry, the better.

There is one exception to that rule. Some forms of specialized casualty insurance are prohibitively expensive. In areas hit by frequent floods or earthquakes, for example, premiums and deductibles are both so high that most homeowners simply can't afford to carry the insurance. They must live with the risk, hoping that their property won't be destroyed when the next catastrophe hits. When the worst does occur, the federal government and some state governments have been known to grant low-interest loans to disaster-struck families so they can rebuild. Some benefits are a form of insurance. For more information, see the section on flood and earthquake insurance later in this chapter.

■ Policy Types

In comparing the different forms of coverage, take note that some cover only named perils, excluding *all* others. Others, however, like the "all-risks" and "comprehensive" forms, cover everything except specified exclusions.

The common forms of casualty insurance include the following:

HO-1: The Basic Policy. This policy provides less coverage than most homeowners need, protecting only your home and possessions against the 11 common perils. No additional losses are included.

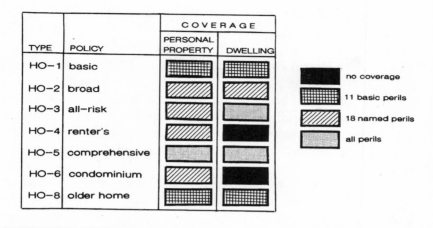

Figure 16.1 Homeowner's Insurance Coverage

HO-2: The Broad Form Policy. Your dwelling and possessions are protected against the 18 listed perils. This is more popular than HO-1 and somewhat more expensive.

HO-3: All-Risk. This is the most widely used form of homeowner's insurance. It includes the "all other" clause, protecting your home against all perils not specifically excluded in the policy. Your personal property is covered only to the extent of the 18 named perils.

HO-4: The Renter's Policy. This protects renters' personal property, plus any improvements they have made at their own expense, against the 18 named perils. The dwelling is not included because it is the owner's responsibility. Renters should carry this form of insurance, since the owner's policy covers *only* the building.

HO-5: Comprehensive. This policy covers everything, meaning all risks except those exclusions actually listed in the policy. It is the most expensive form of homeowner's insurance.

HO-6: The Condominium and Co-op Policy. This policy is designed especially for owners of condos and co-ops, providing protection against losses to personal property and improvements. All-risk coverage is also available under this type of policy. No insurance is included for the building itself, as that insurance is carried by the association and paid for from the monthly fees.

HO-8: Older Homes Policy. This is similar to HO-1 because it covers only the 11 common perils. Some older homes contain fixtures and materials that would be expensive to replace, however, so this policy will replace a damaged older home to serviceable condition, although not necessarily the same condition as before. Both the dwelling and personal property are covered. Figure 16.1 summarizes the coverage for each policy type.

Consult with your insurance agent if you are uncertain about which policy applies in your situation, or about which form of coverage is best in your circumstances. Compare costs and coverage before making a final decision.

■ Cost and Inflation

When shopping for casualty insurance, compare costs for the *same* coverage between companies. You don't get a valid comparison by looking at one company's premium for a comprehensive policy against another's premium for a basic policy.

Keep in mind that there are two ways to value your home and personal property for insurance purposes: actual cash value and replacement cost. The actual cash value is the current value of property based on its cost, *minus* a calculated amount for depreciation. If your policy specifies actual cash values, you will not recover enough in a claim to actually replace the lost possessions.

Replacement cost is different. The insurance provides enough for you to replace items at current cost. However, be aware of a subtle distinction here. If your policy describes claim value as replacement cost, but is limited to some multiplier of actual cash value, you may not be able to recover enough to replace everything. If your policy is a "guaranteed replacement" policy, it should promise to replace all your losses without applying any limitations or calculating any depreciation. In any event, make sure you read your policy and that you understand exactly what you're getting. Guaranteed replacement-cost coverage generally costs about 35 percent more than actual cash-value coverage.

For a higher premium, you can also buy insurance that contains an "inflation guard." That means your property and possessions are covered based on the value at the time you get the insurance, and increased each year to allow for inflation. However, many of these policies have built-in limits on how much increase will be calculated. And expensive items like jewelry, furs, collectibles, and art are not included in the inflation guard provision. For these, you should obtain a separate insurance policy.

■ Limits in Coverage

The standard casualty insurance policy contains limits you should know about. Most common among these are:

> *$500 to $1,000 maximum on:*
> • stamp collections, passports, securities, and manuscripts
> • boats, their motors, and furnishings
> • trailers
> • jewelry, furs, and precious stones
> *$100 to $200 maximum on:*
> • money, precious metals, and coins
> *$1,000 to $2,500 maximum on:*
> • silverware and silver-plated or gold-plated ware
> • firearms

In addition, remember that business assets in the home are *not* covered under any homeowner's insurance policy forms. You need to get a separate policy or ask your agent for a business assets endorsement.

In some high-crime neighborhoods, insurance is high due to burglary and robbery rates. Some lower-than-market rates are available in some areas from the Federal Crime Insurance Program. For information, call the program at 800-638-8780.

■ Flood and Earthquake Insurance

No private insurance coverage is provided for flood or earthquake damage unless you purchase an extra endorsement or rider. In some situations, a separate policy will be needed, depending on the insurance company and rules in the state where you live.

On average, the annual premium for flood insurance is $308, which is more than regular homeowner's insurance in many areas. According to the Federal Emergency Management Agency, of the approximately 11 million buildings in the United States at risk for flood damage, only 2.6 million are insured. For more information about flood insurance, contact the National Flood Insurance Program at 800-638-6620.

The potential loss from earthquakes is at least as serious, although the risk of serious damage is far more likely in certain areas of the country, especially California and Alaska. Rates for earthquake insurance are formidable, costing as much as one-half the amount of premiums for regular coverage, with extremely high deductibles. In California, the deductible may run up to 10 percent of a home's value; in other states, the deductible averages 2 to 5 percent.

If your home is located on a fault line, the insurer could refuse coverage outright. Before buying a home in an earthquake-prone area, investigate the insurability of the home. If the insurance you need is not available, you should think twice about the risks of owning that particular home.

IV

Improving
Your Home

17

Finding a Contractor

Not too long ago, when an American family outgrew its home or simply wanted to add rooms or upgrade their property, the solution was simple: Move. Today, trading up is a luxury in some markets that many families cannot afford. Besides the real estate market, the interest market also limits your ability to move because it could mean replacing a low-interest loan with a high-interest loan. In some states, a move would also trigger an automatic and sometimes significant increase in property taxes.

Since making improvements is often more affordable and practical than moving, many homeowners opt to remain where they are and convert and remodel rather than looking for another home. As a result, the home improvement business is a big industry. According to the U.S. Census Bureau, American homeowners spend more than $45 billion per year on additions and alterations, and another $62 billion on replacements and maintenance.

Like any successful business, the home improvement industry has its share of fraud; caution is advised. According to state contractor boards, homeowners most often report the following types of complaints:

Contractors' poor business practices. For example, when you pay your contractor, the money is used to pay for subcontractors, materials, and other expenses for the *previous* job; the contractor then pays for the materials and subcontractors used on your job with the next project. As a result, whether or not your materials and subcontractors are paid for depends on whether or not the contractor finds another project in the near future. If none are forthcoming, it could mean long delays in completing your work, even if you've paid for it in full (something you should never do until the work is completed). Or the contractor just takes on too much work, and doesn't have the resources to keep promises about deadlines, or does a job hurriedly and not to your satisfaction.

Incompetent work. Sometimes a contractor fails to supervise his or her employees and the work is not up to par. Or the person you hire doesn't have the experience or skill for the job.

Scams. Some fly-by-night operations prey on the unsuspecting homeowner, with the elderly a favorite target. For example, some people are asked to make a large down payment on a job, and that's the last they see of the contractor—and their money.

■ Finding the Right Professional

A contractor is not necessarily the person who will actually do the physical work on your home. As often as not, the contractor merely coordinates crews or subcontracts all or some of the work to other companies. This is common practice, and it works as long as the contractor makes sure that you get what you were promised.

Never hire a contractor who calls you on the telephone, or one who solicits you by mail, or knocks on your door. Many scam artists work on a door-to-door basis. Hiring a contractor should be *your* idea. Look for qualified contractors by checking these sources:

Other customers. Any contractor you choose should be willing to provide you with plenty of local references. The contractor should come highly recommended. If the contractor isn't willing to give you other names, that is a danger signal. Any contractor with happy, satisfied customers would gladly give you their names and numbers. Visit the homes the contractor has worked on (don't settle for photographs), and see the work for yourself. Ask the other customers if they were satisfied with the work, whether it was done on time and on budget, and how long the work took to complete.

Neighbors, friends, and relatives. Do you know anyone who has recently had work done on their house? Chances are good that you do. Ask them for the name of their contractor and, assuming they were pleased with the work, start your inquiry there. Chances of finding a contractor this way are better than if you simply begin calling companies out of the yellow pages.

Subcontractors. Do you know a roofing company, a plumber, or a drywall contractor? These are called subcontractors, and they are hired by contractors to perform the part of a job in which they specialize. They also know all of the general contractors in town. They may be valuable referral sources. But this is not a foolproof method. The subcontractor might merely refer you to the general contractor who uses the subcontractor's company on a lot of jobs. Ask *why* they recommend a particular contractor, and check with more than one source.

State licensing boards. Most states require contractors to operate with a contractor's license or permit. Hire only a legally licensed contractor. You might not have any legal standing to collect in the event an unlicensed contractor doesn't complete your job; even if you do, collecting from an unlicensed contractor will be more difficult. Check with your state licensing board to make sure the contractor is currently licensed. Check with the board even if the contractor gives you a license number or shows you a certificate. You have no way of knowing whether it's current if you don't check. Also, be sure that the license is appropriate for the type of work you want done. About one-third of states have boards just for contractor licenses; the rest have consolidated occupational and professional licensure boards.

Local business groups. The Better Business Bureau can refer you to member contractors in the area. However, if there have been complaints about a BBB member, the local chapter normally will not provide you with the specifics of the case, or disclose the number of complaints.

The Chamber of Commerce will also refer you to its member contractors in the area but, like the BBB, will not provide you with the details of any complaints.

A local chapter of the National Association of Home Builders (NAHB) can refer you to the right type of contractor for the work you need done; local chapters of more specialized associations such as the Remodeler's Council can refer you to members as well. The NAHB is a nationwide association with 185,000 members. For referral to someone in your area, write to NAHB, 1201 15th Street N.W., Washington, DC, 20005, or telephone 800-368-5242.

Other contractors. If you know of a contractor, but that contractor does not do the kind of work you need done, ask for a referral. A professional contractor is likely to be one of your best sources of information.

Real estate agents or lenders. Check with local real estate professionals. They are likely to know all of the local companies that have performed repair work in response to inspections, and will know which ones are the most reliable.

Whatever the source, get as many names as you can. Look for those names that come up time and again. Those companies that do quality work for a competitive price will be referred to you by several people.

■ Estimates and Plans

For comparatively minor jobs, like a basic remodel of a bathroom, uncomplicated sketches will do (more detailed plans might be required by the local building inspector). When preparing an estimate, a contractor will probably prepare a basic sketch for you. Make a copy for yourself, being sure to write down the specifics you've discussed with the contractor. This is necessary because, in getting different estimates from other contractors, you will need to make sure that your comparisons are accurate.

For more complicated projects, like the addition of a room or second story, a set of plans and specifications should be drawn up. These plans will cost money, but they are necessary. Not only do the plans define precisely what will be done and provide the contractor with a document to work from, they also ensure that you know exactly what you're getting and that your concept is what gets put down on paper and, eventually, gets built. You will have to pay for the cost of hiring a draftsman or an architect, depending on the scope of the job. Specifications include complete lists of the type and quality of materials to be used.

Get at least three estimates. If one is extremely low, that isn't necessarily the best way to go. The contractor who underbids probably can't cover costs and make a profit, and will probably not be able to deliver as quality a result as the others would. An exceptionally high estimate might mean you're being offered more than you asked for, or the contractor expects to make a larger profit on the job. If all of the estimates vary considerably, chances are that you have not communicated the same job to each contractor; they aren't really comparable estimates. This is a common mistake. You speak to one contractor who proposes alternatives, and then you discuss an alternative with the next contractor. The only problem is, each one is bidding on a different job, because the selection of design and materials changes with each estimate.

To avoid this problem, write out a description of the job you want done, in as much detail as possible. Prepare your own sketch of what you want. Present this to each contractor, specifying that any additional work or changes to the basic plan should be discussed after they deliver a preliminary estimate. If, during the estimate, anyone makes a suggestion concerning a change, make sure you incorporate that change; call every other contractor who previously estimated the job to modify their estimates according to the changes. Then you will be sure you're getting bids on the same job.

■ Building Permits

Once you select a contractor, sign a contract, and draw up plans, you will need to obtain all applicable licenses and permits required in your area. Every city and county applies its own rules and describes the permitting process with different names, and also has various rules regulating construction and improvements. These various codes and rules fall under the state powers governing health and safety requirements, broadly called "zoning."

You can obtain licenses and permits on your own, or the contractor—

who should know exactly what is required and how to comply—can get them for you. It's likely that plans will be required for a big improvement, and the planning department or building and codes department might have technical questions that are best answered by the contractor. For these reasons, it's probably advisable, not to mention faster, to have the contractor take care of the permitting for you. Make sure you receive copies of all the permits obtained for the job. In many areas, the actual permits are supposed to be prominently posted at the job site, and periodic approvals are conducted by an inspector, ensuring clearance for each phase of the job.

You need to keep the cleared permits. If, years later, you want to sell or refinance, a lender or buyer might ask to see permits for any improvements you have done. Having those documents in a file makes it simple to prove that everything was done "up to code." If you can't prove that the work was done with permits, the improved part of your home might have to be sold "as is," which for many buyers is a big negative.

If you do not go through the permitting process, you could be in for trouble. If your contractor tells you not to worry about getting permits, check for yourself and see if permits are required. Work with a contractor who is willing to go through the system, and not one who believes you can get around it. If, later on, the city or county finds out you performed work without the required permits, you could be fined. Even worse, you might be required to tear down the entire project and do it over with permits.

Be sure you're aware of local rules governing home improvements before you hire a contractor. Even if you're going to trust someone else to go down to city hall in your behalf, you should know in advance what legal requirements and restrictions apply to you. For example, if your improvement will expand your home beyond its current size, do you need a variance from your neighbors? What setbacks are required in the front of your house? Does the zoning conform to the expansion plan you have in mind? A trip to the planning department could be informative and educational.

Find out when building inspectors will be coming to your home to look at the work in progress, and plan to be there. You should know what deficiencies, if any, the inspector discovers. This is a good time to ask questions. For example, let's say an inspector tells your contractor that he or she has to tear out all the electrical wiring because it's not approved under the code, and replace it with the right wiring. Should you be charged for the material and labor? Or should the contractor pay for not knowing better? Make sure you're not being charged for the contractor's careless mistakes.

Without periodic inspections, you will have no way of ensuring that the contractor is following the local code requirements for safety and quality. Don't be swayed by a contractor's argument that working around the required permitting and inspection system is saving you a lot of money. The permits themselves shouldn't cost you more than $100 to $200 for most jobs. That's money well spent to avoid future problems, and to ensure that the job is being done right.

■ Zoning

Another important point to check before you start on your improvement is local zoning. If your building plans conflict with local rules, you will need a variance—meaning you probably will need permission from your neighbors as well as approval from the planning department. You might need to attend a public hearing and make your request on the record, giving any of your neighbors (or any citizen) the opportunity to speak out against your plans. The local planning commission (or other applicable body) will then vote on your request. If it is denied, you will have the right to appeal, but at that point it begins to get expensive and time-consuming. From the planning commission, you might next go to a city or county council, or to a hearing examiner, and ultimately to court. At some point, you might decide that if you're running into resistance getting your variance, it might just be too expensive.

Typical zoning variance issues include adding a second story in an area restricting you to one floor, extending your house or garage toward the street beyond a setback requirement, or expanding your house to add a home office in an area that is supposed to be residential only. Before applying for a variance, walk around the immediate area and talk to your neighbors. Try to get a sense of how people will react to your idea. If you speak to them first, you might not meet any resistance later. However, if they first hear of your plans when they get a notification from the planning commission about a public hearing, you might get a completely different response.

• •

Other Points to Remember

Avoid trouble by following these additional rules:

- Watch out for door-to-door solicitation from anyone offering to perform construction work. A true professional gets business from referrals and advertising, and does not go around ringing doorbells. For example, someone might offer to later give you referral fees for using your home as a model, or doing some work at a discount. These promises never materialize, and making such offers is illegal in many states. Many door-to-door solicitations are really nothing but scams, where someone gets as large a deposit as possible and disappears, or does shoddy work that doesn't improve a problem (or even creates one).
- You should initiate contact. Don't respond to a telephone or in-person offer to look over your home and give you an estimate. It could be a scam or someone trying to case your home for a possible burglary. As with all consumer matters, don't respond to unexpected sales calls.
- Always demand a contractor's license number. If the individual is not licensed, stop the conversation there. If you are given a number, contact the state licensing board and check it out. Make sure it's a current number, and that the number matches the name you were given.
- Know what you're signing. Don't sign any contract or agreement until you've read it completely, and never sign an agreement specifying that most of the money is to be paid up front. Some part of the payment should be payable only upon completion *and* acceptance of the final job. Some documents entitled "estimate" are worded in such a way that they're actually binding contracts. Be sure an estimate specifically says that it is an estimate only and not a contract for work. If a contractor demands you sign something you're not ready to sign, talk to an attorney first.
- Keep a file. Organize it well and make sure every agreement and extra work order gets into the file. Keep copies of all licenses and permits, plans, specifications and drawings, invoices, statements, estimates. By the time a job is done, the file will be full.

• •

▪ Setting up a Payment Schedule

Always ensure that your agreement with the contractor includes a specific payment schedule. It should be in writing and the schedule should make sense. For example, an up-front payment should be enough to cover the purchase price of initially required materials only. Progress payments should be identified logically, based on the percent of the work completed and related expenses (such as labor costs and payments to subcontractors). At least 10 percent should be held until the completion of work, a final inspection by the building inspector, and acceptance by you.

Never agree to payments up-front for anything but specific, identified material costs. These should be strictly limited to the cost of deposits or payments for building materials, fees for drafting plans, building and other permits, and similar payments needed before work can begin.

Coordinating your payments to the contractor's completed work gives you leverage in case of disagreements. In addition, if your contractor is having money problems, this practice protects you and forces the contractor to perform the work promised to you in order to get paid. Don't be put in the position of paying for a previous job and depending on the contractor to receive a deposit from the next person to pay for your materials. As these types of problems escalate, contractors get into financial trouble, eventually finding themselves unable to remain in business. Although not every contractor has trouble managing money, there are enough people out there who do experience these kinds of problems; you need to be careful.

18

Acting as Your Own Contractor

You don't need to hire a contractor if you would rather coordinate and supervise the work yourself. As your own contractor, you can save quite a lot of money because you avoid the general contractor's markups. However, unless you have construction experience, big jobs are best left to the experts.

Many contractors never pick up a hammer. They bid on jobs, keep the books, work out problems on ongoing jobs, order materials, and hire and supervise subcontractors and crews. For this effort, they make a profit on markup—meaning they charge you more than they pay for labor and materials. As your own contractor, you will spend a lot of time running around and doing what the contractor does, but you will cut the costs down considerably.

Experience is not only helpful, it's essential. If you have plumbing experience, for example, remodeling a bath or kitchen will not be as complicated as it will be if you have never touched a pipe. Without experience, you could end up needing a contractor anyhow, probably at much greater expense after the start of the project. This argument applies to any specialized work: masonry, roofing, electrical work, flooring, exterior walls, even installing drywall.

Do-it-yourself home remodeling and improvement is a big business. A large portion of the American public has ventured into this market, not so much as contractors as much as weekend handymen. Many have discovered that jobs are more complex than they appear to be.

■ The Dangers

There's no point in hiring a contractor for small maintenance jobs. Most people can figure out how to put on their own weather stripping, paint a room, or install a door handle. But if you're adding a room or putting in a swimming pool, you'd better be prepared to work with a contractor.

The primary reason for beginning a home improvement on your own will be to save money, unless you simply enjoy doing your own work. Savings can be substantial, but you should first decide whether it's worth the time you will spend working on your own. Consider the special pitfalls of the do-it-yourself handyman:

Inexperience costs money. Unless you're versatile and skilled in the many steps involved in a major home improvement, you may have no idea what you're in for. You may not have an accurate idea of what the project will eventually cost. At worst, you could end up with a financial disaster and an unfinished job. Doing the work incorrectly means higher expense and delays.

It takes more time. Assuming that you will be working in your free time—evenings and weekends—the work will take longer than it would for a contractor. If a contractor would take two full weeks to complete the job, it may take you several months on a part-time schedule. This also means more noise, dust, and inconvenience for your family.

Everything is up to you. You need to complete the project on your own, meaning you need to negotiate with subcontractors, buy and coordinate materials, draft your own plans, deal with the planning department, arrange and schedule inspections, arrange financing, and schedule the whole job from beginning to end.

Financing is more difficult. If you will need to obtain a loan to finance your project, many lenders will be hesitant to work with you as a do-it-yourself handyman. Some refuse outright. Too many lenders have seen these projects fail, cost twice what they should have cost, or end up in a default situation. Because the lender's risks are greater when you do the work yourself, you will have to be able to demonstrate that you have the skill and experience to do the work.

Your life is disrupted. Whereas a contractor may disrupt your family's quiet enjoyment, doing it yourself could be a worse experience. The stress of noise, dust, construction materials, and financial strain is worsened when a big job extends over several weeks or months. Too many people have found this approach far less rewarding than they'd hoped when they started out.

■ Coordinating Subcontractors

When you act as your own general contractor, you can farm out the entire job and never have to lift a finger of your own. But there will be plenty for you to do, just in estimating, ordering supplies, and coordinating the schedule. These management tasks are the most critical aspects of the job.

When you hire subcontractors, it's best to exercise the same level of care you need when working with a general contractor. This means ensuring the contract has everything you need to protect yourself, like a schedule of payments, a definition of responsibilities, and a schedule of the work itself. This caution has to be exercised with each and every subcontractor—for a major improvement, that could mean working with 15 or so different people. Even if you use only six—a plumber, an electrician, a carpenter, a floor installer, a painter, and a drywall contractor—it can still be a formidable organizational task.

As an example, let's say you're remodeling a bathroom—not expanding it, just replacing existing fixtures and relocating a few pipes, installing a new floor, adding a window, and painting the entire room. After your plans have been approved, all bids received from subcontractors, and contracts signed—assuming that you have ordered all of the fixtures needed for the job and have been given a firm delivery date—you can begin to schedule the work. But the work is still contingent upon the delivery date working out and your various subcontractors showing up when you schedule them.

Because you are not certain how much time to allot for each phase of the job, you generously estimate that the job will take about two weeks. A general contractor probably could complete the job in a few days, but since you're not sure you add extra time.

You plan to tear out the old fixtures and the existing wall and floors over a weekend. No problem—that is, until you discover that you don't have the right tools to detach the sink, toilet, and bathtub connections. Not only that, you discover that you don't know how to turn off your water supply. Then you realize you can't haul off the old bathtub by yourself.

By now, of course, you have begun tearing the room apart. Is this your only bathroom? If so, you have problems and it's only the first day of the job, not to mention it may be the weekend. Should you move your family into a hotel or go live with relatives for a couple of weeks? Or can you schedule the job tightly enough so that facilities will be out of working order for only a few days?

Then a subcontractor arrives, and you discover that he doesn't have the right parts or equipment to complete the job either. Those parts have to be ordered, and that will take at least two days. That means everything else has to be pushed up because the schedule is thrown off.

From this example, you can see that, from the very beginning, many things can go wrong with your job. There is no shortage of potential problems.

■ Your Extra Liability

Even if your job proceeds like clockwork, you have another risk: increased liability. What if someone gets hurt on the job? This is a risk you assume even when working with a general contractor, but that contractor's experience and knowledge make such accidents less likely to occur. If a subcontractor is injured in your home because you did some preliminary work incorrectly and created a hazard, you may be liable for damages. For example, let's say you tear up your old floor and fail to warn a subcontractor, who walks into the room, trips and falls through the flooring, and breaks an arm. Or you stack materials carelessly, and a heavy appliance falls over, seriously injuring a worker. You would be liable.

Remember, as the general contractor, if you hire a subcontractor, negotiating the cost of work, you need to ensure that the individual or company carries liability insurance and worker's compensation. If you hire workers to be paid by the hour, you're required to provide your own worker's compensation coverage, and to withhold social security, federal and state income taxes, and disability and unemployment insurance—and to report and pay those withheld amounts to the government. It's complicated.

■ Do-It-Yourself Checklist

If you decide to act as your own contractor, follow these steps to prevent the most common pitfalls:

Check with your lender. Find out before you begin whether your lender will be willing to finance a home improvement if you will act as your own contractor. Line up your financing before you begin and, if possible, include a contingency fund. A home equity loan is excellent for this purpose. (See Chapter 19.)

Check subcontractor references. Go through a complete and thorough review of all subcontractor references, just as you would when hiring a general contractor. Ask for references, check and verify state licenses, and get written estimates before signing anything. Get several estimates to make an informed decision about which subcontractor to hire.

Draw plans and specifications. A general contractor can work from partial drawings and explain to a crew exactly what needs to be done. If the contractor works with the same people every day, communication like this has been perfected. But when you act as your own contractor, you can't afford to leave anything to chance. You need to have plans drawn up by a professional draftsman or architect, and you also need to write out a complete specifications list.

Get required permits. Check with your local planning department to find out which permits are required for your job. Obtain all permits before you start your work, and be sure to allow for building inspections in your schedule. Don't think of being your own contractor as an excuse to work around the permitting process.

Draw up a job schedule. Plan each and every phase of the job. Consult with subcontractors to determine how much time they will need, and allow extra time at each phase for delays.

Check insurance risks. Make sure you're completely covered for any liabilities while work is underway. A professional subcontractor should have insurance, but check to make sure your risks are also covered.

Supervise. Spend time supervising your subcontractors while work is underway. Make sure arrival and start dates are honored, and that suppliers make their deliveries when promised.

Allow for inconveniences. Think about the disruptions to your normal family life that will occur while work is underway. You will have strangers in your home, often as early as 7 A.M., walls will be opened up, dust will settle on everything, and the entire day will be characterized by constant noise.

Schedule payments with work. All payments to subcontractors should be agreed to by written contract and drawn up in advance. Don't vary from the schedule, and always leave a portion owing pending your final acceptance of the work. Be sure the building inspector also approves the work *before* the subcontractor is paid in full.

Check subcontractors' suppliers. Just because you're your own contractor, you're not protected from a mechanic's lien. Check directly with all of your subcontractors' suppliers to ensure they have been paid.

19

Financing an Improvement

If you are contemplating asking for financing for a self-contracting job, remember that the lender's decision will be based on three important factors:

1. The amount of equity in your home.

2. Your credit history and current income level.

3. The type of improvement and whether you'll do the work yourself or hire a contractor.

The equity you have built up is critical to the lender, who is interested in ensuring that you have a stake in repaying your loan. Having equity makes it very unlikely that you will default on your loan.

When you first purchase your home, lenders require that you have some equity, often as much as 20 percent. They will then be willing to finance the remaining 80 percent of the purchase price. For example, if your new home is valued at $125,000, the lender may offer to finance $100,000 and require you to make a down payment of $25,000, or a combination of cash and a second mortgage.

When you undertake an improvement, the same rules apply, although not necessarily at the same percentages. The formula might vary. For example, if you're planning to finance a $25,000 home improvement, that would raise the value of your house to $150,000. A lender may be willing to finance up to 80 percent of that value, or $120,000. Subtracting the balance of your mortgage from the $120,000 (let's assume your mortgage by this time is $97,000), you can arrive at the amount the lender will be willing to finance in this way:

Value of home after improvement	$150,000
80 percent	120,000
Less: current mortgage balance	- 97,000
Maximum financing available	$ 23,000

In this example, you will need to come up with $2,000 to make up the difference. The lender's rules, though, won't always be so easy to calculate. For example, your lender may want to discount the improved value of your home, to be conservative or simply because lenders might believe it will take time for the full cost to be realized in market value. There is some historical justification for such approaches, since many improvements don't add value to your home immediately. If the lender believes, for example, that the $25,000 improvement will add only $20,000 to your home's value immediately, the formula will have to be adjusted:

Value of home after improvement	$145,000
80 percent	116,000
Less: current mortgage balance	- 97,000
Maximum financing available	$ 19,000

In that case, you would need to come up with $6,000 cash to pay for your $25,000 improvement. It's tougher to get a lender to agree to finance a home improvement loan if you plan to do the work yourself, no matter how high your equity. If you're an experienced craftsman and you've done a lot of renovation work in the past, furnish the lender with proof of your skills: photographs of your work or references from other people, for example.

The question of adequately estimating the cost of work to be done is also critical to the lender. If your estimate turns out to be low and you run out of money, the lender will probably be stuck with an unfinished job. That reduces the value of the property, making matters even worse. If, on the other hand, a hired contractor provides you with a written, firm estimate, that binds the price and gives the lender assurance that the equity interest will not be affected. That's a powerful argument for granting the financial application.

■ Finding the Right Financing

Whether you do your own work or hire a contractor, you have several possible sources for financing the project:

Cash. If you have cash, that takes away a lot of pressure. You will save thousands of dollars you would otherwise pay in interest for any job costing more than a couple of thousand dollars. But don't deplete your emergency reserves in the process; keep some ready money for unexpected emergencies.

Insurance policies. If you have a cash-value whole life policy, you can borrow your cash reserves at a relatively low-interest rate.

Credit union. This may be a good source for a loan. Ask your credit union for rates on home improvement loans. They may be competitive with other lenders' rates.

Contractors. Some contractors might be able to get you a lower-than-market rate through a lender with whom they do a lot of work. Under such arrangements, progress payments are set up to be paid directly to the contractor, and you might not have as much control or leverage as you do when paying the contractor directly.

Finance companies. You can get a home improvement loan from a finance company, but in most cases that will also mean paying high interest rates.

Credit cards. You can finance a home improvement with credit cards, but interest rates could be very high—unless you can get a card with a low rate, a common introductory offer made by credit card companies.

Savings and loan associations. The S&L is a popular source for many types of financing, including home improvement loans. Many will carry a first mortgage for as long as 30 years but limit home-improvement loans to a 15-year term.

Banks. Terms vary from one bank to another. Many are willing to finance purchases of homes or refinance loans but don't want to touch the home improvement loan market; others compete directly with savings and loans or credit unions, offering competitive terms.

The federal government. Government loans are available for improvements to your home at competitive rates, usually with some restrictions. Some programs place a ceiling on the amount you can borrow, or strictly limit the purpose of the loan. Such programs may be available to you through the Veterans Administration, the Federal Housing Administration, or other agencies. For example, if you live in a rural area, a home improvement loan might be arranged through the Farmers Home Administration, but only if your income is relatively low. Each agency applies its own set of rules.

State governments. Most states offer home improvement loan programs at below-market rates, usually with restrictions on use of proceeds, or only in certain circumstances. For example, if your improvement results from flood damage, you might qualify for a state-sponsored low-interest loan. Check your telephone book under state housing agencies for more information.

Private sources. You can borrow money from a private investor, a family member, or a friend. Or you may arrange a second mortgage through a mortgage company, with terms ranging between 3 or 5 years, all the way up to 15 years. Expect rates to be higher than those available from other lenders.

Equity lines of credit. A bank, savings institution, brokerage house, or other lender may allow you a line of credit you can use in any way you want. The line is secured by your home equity. The home equity line is discussed in more detail in the next section.

■ Home Equity Loans

Your home is a valuable asset, as lenders are well aware. Currently, most banks, savings and loan associations, and even credit unions offer lines of credit as an alternative to loaning outright. These lines of credit are secured by the equity in your home.

You may have seen ads on television or in the newspaper for products advising you to "put your equity to work" or "use the money laying idle in your home" for other purposes. And you may feel guilty about not taking advantage of that equity. But remember: Putting your equity to work really means borrowing money secured by the equity. Borrowed money has to be paid back eventually. It is not a good idea to use home equity for vacations, debt consolidation, and other non-permanent reasons. However, your equity is well used for financing

● ●

Refinancing Your Home

You can refinance your home in order to pay for a large-scale improvement, but before you do, consider these important points:

- You shouldn't refinance if your first mortgage is at a fixed rate lower than current market rates. Look instead for a second mortgage, and don't give up that low fixed rate.
- Be sure you can afford the payments and that you understand the terms of the new loan. For example, with rare exception, you should not give up a fixed-rate loan for a variable-rate loan if you plan to remain in your home for longer than the next five years (which is likely if you're thinking of making improvements). Lenders carrying fixed-rate loans below current market will gladly trade them in and may even make attractive offers to entice you, but you're better off not taking the bait.
- Be prepared for a prepayment penalty if you're paying off an older mortgage—worthwhile if you're getting a good break on the mortgage rate. Even so, the penalty might mean you'll need a few years to break even on your savings.
- If your new loan includes cash you need to pay for an improvement, be sure it's enough. Remember, you'll need money for closing costs for the refinance, including points, appraisal fees, credit reports, title insurance, and—if applicable—the prepayment penalty.
- You can reduce interest by taking out a separate loan just for the improvement and paying if off over a shorter period than your existing first mortgage. The sooner you pay off a loan, the lower your interest expense—as long as you can afford the payment schedule on your budget.

● ●

home improvements, since they enhance the value of your investment.

When Congress outlawed "consumer interest" several years ago, the change triggered the home equity line of credit industry. Because mortgage interest is deductible, the plan was simple. Pay off auto loans and credit cards with an equity line of credit that enables you to deduct your interest. Many people follow that plan, only to replace old debt with new debt. As a consequence, they go more deeply into debt rather than solving their problems.

To show how dramatically the home equity market has grown in recent years, consider this: According to the Board of Governors of the Federal Reserve System, in December 1988, American consumers owed $40 billion in home equity loans. Four years later, the amount had nearly doubled, to $73 billion.

A traditional mortgage allows you a fixed amount of money for the purchase of a home. But with an equity line of credit, the lender makes a maximum amount available to you that you can use as you please and when you please. You only pay interest on the money you actually take out. Since many people use their equity lines frequently, they are similar to credit card accounts, with established maximum balances. You have to repay the minimum each month, but you can repay anything above the minimum without penalty. Interest is calculated based on average daily balances.

As an example of how the equity line is calculated, let's say your lender applies the rule that you cannot borrow more than 80 percent of your equity. If your house is worth $150,000 and you owe $97,000 on your mortgage, your available equity is:

Market value of the home	$150,000
80 percent maximum debt	120,000
Less: current mortgage	- 97,000
Balance available	$ 23,000

In this example, a lender may grant you an equity line of credit up to $23,000. Using such an account turns your home equity into a type of credit card. You will usually be given a supply of checks that you can use as freely as you like, perhaps too freely for many people. You are required to repay a portion of the loan each month. (It's good to remember that the higher the amount borrowed, the higher the monthly minimum payment will be as well.)

This form of credit is seductive. It's too easy to glide into debt. Over time, the equity in your home can be eroded by high interest payments. In some arrangements, you're required to pay interest only. As a result, over time, you're paying a lot for borrowing the money. Home equity loan interest rates tend to be higher than home mortgage rates, often averaging one to three points above the prime rate. In addition, the interest is usually variable. (If market rates climb, so does your repayment obligation and interest expense.)

At some point, probably between five and ten years later, the whole loan comes due. (It's important to note that many lenders have the right to demand the balance of the home equity loan at any time.) When it is due, you might be strapped, perhaps even forced to sell your home just to meet the obligation. If you have used the equity line of credit for vacations, new cars, and debt consolidation, you could end up with a huge debt and little to show for it.

The equity-based line of credit is designed by lenders to realize great profits, all secured by equity in your home. The lender runs little risk compared with what you face if you misuse the privilege of "easy" access to money. You should avoid using an equity line of credit unless you're able to exercise great control and discipline in managing your money.

■ The Dangers of Overimproving

If you're improving your home mainly for your own enjoyment and comfort, that's one thing. However, if you're remodeling with the idea of increasing market value, perhaps anticipating selling in a few years, you should be aware of the dangers of overimproving.

"Conformity" is important in real estate. As a general rule, a house should be of a similar size, with similar features (number of bedrooms and bathrooms), located on a similarly sized lot as other homes in the area. If one home is exceptionally large, with more and better features, the owner is not likely to realize full value upon sale because the nonconformity of the home holds its market value down.

A neighborhood generally has a natural ceiling on the prices of homes. For example, if a typical three-bedroom, two-bath home in your area sells for $115,000, with a maximum of $135,000 for the nicest homes (based on sales during the past two years), there is probably little or no investment value in improving your home very far beyond the ceiling value. If your house is currently valued at $120,000, adding a den, a swimming pool, an extra bedroom, or a family room is not likely to increase the house's market value very much, if at all. Your total costs might add up to $50,000, but that does not automatically mean your house will increase in value dollar for dollar. Conformity controls the maximum you would realize upon sale. Value is set by neighborhoods and general condition more than by the amount of money you put into improvements.

Some improvements have their own built-in limitations, in addition to not conforming with the neighborhood. A swimming pool, for example, can inhibit a sale. Many buyers don't want pools; a pool increases your homeowner's liability insurance. Families with small children may view the pool as an unacceptable danger; others won't want to pay the high cost of monthly upkeep. Some buyers may prefer a yard, in which case your house would be crossed off the list of serious prospects because it has a pool. Similarly, greenhouses, elaborate landscaping, and solar power systems do not appeal to the average buyer, making your house more difficult to sell.

In general, remodeled kitchens and bathrooms are the improvements most likely to add immediate value to your home. Resale value is likely to improve dollar for dollar, sometimes with a premium. Kitchens and bathrooms are the most utilized parts of the house, and updated, renovated features appeal greatly to home buyers. The addition of a second bath in a one-bath home is especially valuable on the market.

■ Energy Considerations

You can also save money by keeping in mind how much a home improvement will cost or save in future energy bills. A new living room with an unusually high ceiling may be an elegant touch, but over the years your heating and cooling bills may make you think twice about the value of the improvement. A future buyer might have the same concerns.

Beware of other energy-inefficient improvements that, in the long run, will cost you much more money, including:

- Too many windows. Glass is poor insulation all year round. If they face south or west, they catch the hottest sunlight; if they

face north, they tend to let in the cold. Go with double-pane glass.
- Skylights and sliding doors. These must be placed and set with precision, with high-quality materials rated high for energy efficiency.
- Open spaces. A large room without doors and other separators or dividers takes longer to heat and cool and costs more.

An improvement can also have unexpected effects on the rest of your home. For example, one family expanded their living space by doubling the size of their family room and adding a new dining area. In the process, they removed a wall separating the kitchen from the original, smaller family room. Within a year, they realized that they had built in a number of expensive features. The family area, now twice its original size, was difficult to heat and cool, and it was an area where the family spent a lot of time. In the warmer months, heat from cooking in the kitchen made the family room and other first-floor areas unbearable with the original kitchen wall gone. In colder weather, their new sliding door and added windows created drafty, cold rooms throughout the main floor. In fact, the heating and cooling bills were so much higher that they ended up rebuilding the kitchen wall.

Another family remodeled their bathroom and, in the process, covered the room's only window, replacing it with a vent. The vent kept heat and moisture to a minimum, but the family missed the window. During the hot summer months, they'd always left the window open in the evening, allowing a cool breeze to waft through their bedrooms. Without the ventilation provided by the bathroom window, the bedrooms tended to become stuffy and hot, so air-conditioning was finally installed. The moral of the story: Even a small renovation, undertaken without sufficient thought and study, can add to energy costs and make your living space less comfortable.

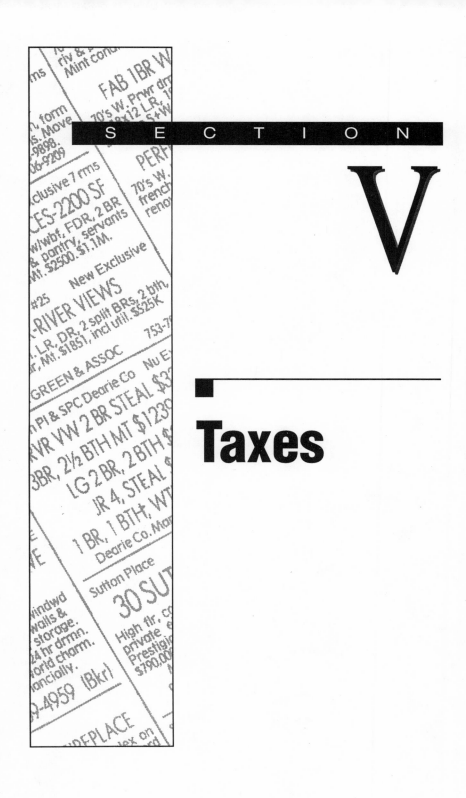

SECTION

V

Taxes

20

Keeping Track of Your Investment

Owning your own home means having to keep records—a lot of records that have to be kept for a very long time. You will need these records to document tax deductions or to calculate the eventual profit upon selling your home. The IRS advises keeping documents for any particular year at least three years after the filing deadline for that year. (That means April 15 in most instances; but if you file for an extension, the deadline gets extended, too.) The three-year rule is a good one to remember. But when it comes to your home and the records about purchase price, improvements, and closing costs, you will need to keep your file active for much longer.

You can simplify your record keeping to a degree. For example, most mortgage lenders provide you with a monthly payment record that shows the total payment, the breakdown between interest and principal, as well as payments for impounds (for homeowner's insurance and property taxes, if you have impounds included with your payment). These monthly stubs can be thrown away at the end of each year, when your lender provides you with the annual summary.

If you replace one homeowner's insurance policy with another, there's no need to keep the old policy; it can be discarded. Upon completion of a home improvement, you can get rid of unused estimates and plans, minor correspondence between you and contractors or suppliers, and other miscellaneous paperwork that does not relate to the cost of the improvement or satisfaction of your debt to the contractor.

Following is a list of the typical documents every homeowner accumulates over the years. There are three broad classifications: ownership, insurance and mortgages, and improvements.

■ Ownership Records

Legal description. This is a complete description, usually about one paragraph long, describing the exact location and dimensions of your property that are referenced to an entry in a plat book, which is part of your county's permanent property records. Typically, the property description identifies the county, the exact location in reference to a marker, and the length and direction of your property lines.

Closing statement. This is a summary of the price you paid for your property, including prorated taxes, interest, insurance, rent, utilities, and all filing fees, lender charges, processing fees, title insurance charges, and recording fees; it concludes with the amount of money deposited at closing (by the buyer) or due to be paid (to the seller).

Deed of trust or mortgage. This is a document transferring legal title and rights to your property to the lender, to be reconveyed upon satisfaction of the debt.

Loan disclosure statement. This is the lender's summary showing the amount you are borrowing, the interest rate, and the APR (annual interest rate, the compounded rate including prorated annual shares of lender fees). This detailed information has to be provided to you in writing as a requirement of the Federal Truth in Lending Act. It includes the total dollar amount of all payments and the amount and date of each monthly payment.

Promissory note. This is a note signed by the buyer acknowledging obligation to repay the lender.

Title company's preliminary report. This summarizes the results of the title search, including a listing of all liens. It usually includes current loans and notes, mechanics' liens, property taxes due and payable, and any other obligations, such as options on the property. The report normally comes out two weeks or more before closing date.

Title insurance update. Immediately before closing, the title company will check the record again, to ensure that no last-minute liens appear on the property.

Title insurance policy. This is a contract between you and the title company. It states that any undisclosed liens will be paid by the company, protecting you as the new owner. The policy is paid for at closing, and it remains in force for as long as you own the home.

Deposit receipt. This is a document signed by both buyer and seller upon initiation of the contract (when the offer is accepted). It includes the terms and contingencies of the contract.

Pest-control inspection report. This is the report issued by the inspector. You should always receive a copy, which you should keep in your file. It describes any infestations or damage, and recommends corrective action.

Other inspection reports. The reports of home inspection companies and any other required inspections should be provided to you at closing. Keep these on file.

Warranties. Any contracts or promises made in writing by real estate agents, sellers, or inspectors should be kept in your file.

Neighborhood plan and zoning ordinance. These documents are not provided for you; you have to get them on your own. A neighborhood plan shows you how the whole area is zoned. More important, it discusses plans for the future. For example, the plan might reveal that your local government planners intend to turn your quiet street into the next major traffic artery, which will lower property values. We highly recommend that you get a neighborhood plan and read it thoroughly when you are investigating neighborhoods. Keep it in a file with your zoning ordinance, which discloses exactly what type of zoning activities are allowed in your area.

■ Insurance and Mortgage Records

Homeowner's insurance policy. This is the policy currently in effect insuring you against property liabilities and casualties. Discard older, outdated policies as they are updated or replaced.

Mortgage insurance policies. These are policies insuring that your family, in the event of your death or disability, will be able to pay off the mortgage and keep the family home.

Property tax statements. These statements are mailed to you from the local assessor's office, breaking down your semiannual and annual tax obligations for the property. They show the computation of the tax, the assessed value, the legal description or an abbreviated version, and the amount and dates of the tax that is coming due.

Your property tax bills are paid directly to your county treasurer or other official. If you have agreed to allow your lender to collect impounds, the lender then takes an estimated one-twelfth of the tax liability each month, making payments to your county in your behalf. You can request that impounds not be taken, in which case you will be responsible for paying your taxes directly, usually twice per year in lump sums. You may prefer having your lender collect and pay this tax for you.

Mortgage payment statements. These monthly stubs or summaries show your account number, address, amount due date, and usually a breakdown between principal and interest. Some lenders provide a very helpful summary of year-to-date interest and the current principal balance. You can discard monthly records once you receive an annual summary from the lender.

Reconveyance notice. This is a copy of the notice filed by a lender once you have fully repaid the debt. Be sure you get a notice of reconveyance, even for minor second mortgages. Also, make sure it is recorded at your county recorder's office, to remove the lien on your property.

Assessment and improvement notices. These are notices sent to you by local authorities or the planning commission, announcing upcoming improvements. These include installing or upgrading utilities, putting in sidewalks, storm drains, or curbs. You will be charged for your share of the project, but these projects often also add to the market value of the property.

Area assessor's map. This is a copy of the page from your county's plat book, showing property divisions in your neighborhood. It will be given to you, usually free of charge or for a small copying fee, upon request. You will also get a free copy when assessments are announced or when public notices are sent out because someone nearby wants a variance.

Appraisal reports. Always ask for a copy of the appraisal. If you paid for it, you're entitled to see the report. In it the appraiser documents his or her calculations estimating the value of your home.

■ Improvements

Plans and specifications. The description of materials and the drawings of work done are important documents that should be kept.

Building and other permits. Keep all permits for work done to your property.

Inspection records. Whenever a building inspector approves portions of work done and the final job itself, a notation is usually made on a permanent record posted at the job site. Keep this record in your file.

Estimates. Keep all written estimates submitted by contractors that you ultimately accept. These are useful for calculating the cost of similar projects in the future, and could be important for resolving any financial disputes you might have with your contractor.

Contract. Keep all agreements, including change orders, signed by you and your contractor.

Record of payments. This is a summary of all invoices or statements, canceled checks, and other documents referring to your agreement on the payment schedule with your contractor. If the contractor issues a monthly statement, it can be kept in place of invoices.

Preliminary lien notices. These are mailed to you by each subcontractor and supplier. They should be kept in your file for future cross-reference to lien releases.

Lien releases. These releases are sent to you as each subcontractor or supplier is paid. You should also get an unconditional lien release from the contractor.

Notice of completion. This is a notice filed and recorded at your county office, announcing the completion of work on your home improvement. Recording this notice begins the running of a time limit for anyone who wants to file a lien.

■ Other Home Expenses

You should also hold on to all records pertaining to the maintenance and upkeep of your home and its systems. Include documents related to painting; landscaping; repairs to plumbing, electrical, heating and air-conditioning systems; and the purchase of fixtures such as carpeting, appliances, garage door openers, and sprinkler systems.

Keep records for all of the household expenses until they become obsolete through replacement. Whereas none of these are deductible (unless you use part of your home for business or rental), you will have a permanent record of all warranties and guarantees. In the event of a casualty, these may become critical, because you will need to estimate the cost of replacement for anything that is lost.

When it is time to sell, a buyer will also be interested in seeing proof that you have kept all systems maintained and in working order. It is helpful, too, if you keep a record of monthly utility costs. Buyers often have no idea what it costs to heat or cool a house, and having copies of recent utility bills helps establish the recent history of those costs by season.

21

How Home Sales Are Taxed

One of the primary benefits of owning your own house, condo, or co-op is that, with proper planning, you probably will not be required to pay income tax on the profit you gain from selling your home. This is true at least on the federal level, while each state applies rules and regulations of its own.

The boon for homeowners is found in the tax laws. You are allowed to defer the taxes due on the profit from selling your home as long as that home is classified as your "principal residence." That means you have to live there for at least three out of the five years immediately before you sell. This is true whether it's a single-family house, a condo, or a co-op. As long as you buy or build another home within two years, your profits are deferred until you sell that subsequent house. In fact, it's not a choice. You are *required* to defer the tax if you meet all of the qualifications.

Another major benefit is available to anyone aged 55 or more. A once-in-a-lifetime exclusion is allowed up to $125,000 in profits from selling your home. For example, if you buy a house for $100,000 and later sell it for $225,000, the difference, or profit of $125,000 is not taxed—as long as you're over 55. But you can use this benefit only once.

■ Capital Gains

We all pay taxes on income from salaries and wages, investment income, self-employment income, tips, alimony, and gains from the sale of property.

Capital gains are classified as gains on items like homes or investments. As of the date this book went to press, capital gains taxes are being debated in Congress and changes in the future are likely. The history of capital gains is an on-again, off-again story. So much economic impact comes from taxing policy that no one knows for certain what the real impact will be if the capital gains tax laws are changed. However, among ideas being seriously discussed by our lawmakers is a reduction in the tax rate for capital gains and, as some favor, abolishing the tax altogether. There is also some discussion about removing the mortgage-interest deduction.

These decisions will all affect the way you are taxed on the sale of a house, condo, or co-op. If you are planning to sell your home in the future, you should consult—in advance—with a tax planner or accountant to ensure that you understand the tax consequences and benefits of your decision. Find out the current status of capital gains rules and how they will affect you.

As of this book's press date, capital gains on your principal residence are taxed, subject to deferral rules. That means only that the tax itself is not paid until later, not that the transaction is not taxed. However, losses on the sale of a residence are *not* deductible.

■ Once-in-a-Lifetime Exclusion Rule

The rationale for the once-in-a-lifetime rule is that people beginning to plan for their retirement should not be penalized with a large tax bill at the same time that they're starting to live on a fixed income. That would take away a large portion of their profits and harm the elderly financially in too many cases. Under current tax law, the provision allows you to exclude up to $125,000 of profits from the sale of your principal residence. If you are married, but you and your spouse own property separately, each of you is allowed only $62,500. If you are married but filing separately, the same rule applies. In other words, married people have to split the privilege, whereas single people get the full $125,000.

You must be 55 or older on the date of the sale, and you must have owned and lived in the home as a principal residence for at least three out of the past five years, calculated to end on the day the sale closes. For a married couple holding property jointly and filing a joint return during the year of the sale, either the husband or the wife can satisfy the age requirement as well as the ownership rule.

Example: A single man marries at the age of 54. He has been living in his house for more than three years. His new wife is 51. The year after they are married, they decide to sell the house. Because the husband is 55 and has lived there more than three out of the last five years, the couple meets the requirements—even though the wife meets neither the age nor the residence tests.

One problem can arise in this situation if, for example, the man's new wife was already over 55 *and* she had previously used the exclusion on a separate property. In that case, the provision cannot be used again. In this situation, some advance planning would pay off. As a single man who has not yet used the exclusion, the man could sell the house before getting married and legally would be entitled to the $125,000 once-in-a-lifetime exclusion.

Here's how it works when a single person or a married couple are fully qualified. Let's say a house is sold for $184,000, less closing costs of $13,000. Net proceeds in this case are $171,000. The home originally cost $63,000 plus closing costs of $2,000, equaling the adjusted basis of $65,000. The profit is $106,000:

Sales price		$184,000
Less: Closing costs		13,000
Adjusted sales price		$171,000
Less: original cost	$63,000	
Plus closing costs	2,000	
Adjusted purchase price		65,000
Profit		$106,000

If the seller in this example was over 55 and had lived in the home as a principal residence for at least three out of the last five years before the sale, the profit is entirely excluded from tax. This also assumes that the owner had not previously used the exclusion, and that his or her spouse had not claimed it either. As long as the profit is at or below $125,000, it escapes tax.

You cannot take advantage of this provision for any portion of your home that is used as an office or rented out to someone else. If you use part of your home for these purposes, you are required to pay tax on the profit of that portion of the home not used as a principal residence. Sale proceeds then have to be broken down between residential and nonresidential uses. This is usually done on a percentage basis calculated by square feet.

Example: Let's say you bought a home in 1990 for $100,000 and regularly used one room as an office, claiming a home-office deduction on your tax return each year and also claiming depreciation for that part of the home. In 1996, you sell your home for $160,000. The square feet of the total living space is 2,400 feet, and the home office measures 300 feet, or one-eighth of the total. Your gain on each portion is broken down as:

Residence portion:
Amount realized ($\frac{7}{8}$ x $160,000)		$140,000
Basis ($\frac{7}{8}$ of $100,000)		87,500
Gain realized		$ 52,500

Office portion:
Amount realized ($\frac{1}{8}$ of $160,000)		$ 20,000
Basis ($\frac{1}{8}$ of $100,000)	$12,500	
Less: depreciation, $5\frac{1}{2}$ years	1,250	
Adjusted basis		11,250
Gain realized		$ 8,750

When you use part of your home as an office, the calculation of depreciation involves several steps. First of all, you can't deduct the value of land. You can estimate the land's value by looking at your property tax statement, where your assessed value is broken down between land and improvements (on the home). Apply that percentage to your purchase price.

For our illustration, we assumed that land was one-half the value of the property. Therefore, starting with the total basis of $12,500, the owner would be allowed to deduct depreciation based on only half of that total, or $6,250.

Next, we applied the annual depreciation rate. Under current federal law, you are allowed to depreciate residential real estate over $27\frac{1}{2}$

years. To calculate depreciation, we first divided the allowable basis of $6,250 by the term allowed, $27\frac{1}{2}$ years; we then multiplied that by $5\frac{1}{2}$, the period the room was used as an office:

$6,250 / 27.5 = $227 per year

$227 x 5.5 years = $1,248.50

This demonstrates that the homeowner would have to pay tax on $8,750 of gain on the sale, even if the total profit did not exceed the exclusion value of $125,000 in total profit. The same calculation would be applied for use of a part of your home as a rental.

As you can see, the nonpersonal use of your home greatly reduces the value of an exclusion. Of course, if the gain is well over $125,000, you might still get the full benefit. There are some tax planning ideas you can apply if you rent out part of your home or have a home office, and you plan to sell in the future and will qualify for the exclusion. You have the option of extending depreciation over a longer period than the 27.5 years, meaning the taxable basis will be smaller because there is less depreciation to apply.

Before setting up any portion of your home as an office or for rental income, consult with your tax adviser. Discuss all tax planning considerations before making your final decision.

■ Tax Deferral on Sale

The second substantial tax benefit for homeowners is available to anyone who sells their principal residence. If you buy or build a new home within two years from the date of sale, the entire profit is deferred—in most cases.

The exclusions to this provision are identical to those for the once-in-a-lifetime exclusion. You do not defer the gain on any part of your home used as an office or to generate rental income.

Capital gains are usually computed as being fully taxable. The adjusted sales price, minus the adjusted purchase price, is the taxable gain.

An important qualifying rule: You can defer taxes on gains as many times as you like, as long as you don't do it more than once during any two-year period. If you do, the latest sale is deferred, but you'll have to go back and amend your tax return to report the profit on the earlier sale. This provision applies *only* to your residence.

■ Trading Up

Most homeowners eventually want a bigger home. Families grow, meaning there is a greater need. And incomes expand, enabling a family to live in a nicer, newer, larger home. The tax laws are set up to make it easier for you to trade up without having to give up part of your equity in taxes. Trading up is attractive because:

- It enables you to defer all of the gain on sale of your previous home (as long as your new home costs more than the adjusted sales price of your old home).
- It allows you to create a larger investment base for retirement, or for future profits in selling a home.
- It allows you and your family to improve your lifestyle and comfort in the home environment.
- It provides for improved housing conditions as your income grows, without being penalized by income taxes.

It's quite conceivable that you will buy and sell several homes during your lifetime. Few people remain in one place for long, and the average first-time buyer stays less than five years. It's also possible to move from one home to another several times, make a profit with every home, and *never* pay taxes—legally.

Let's say your first home is purchased when you're 28 and sold when you're 33. You live in your second home for 10 years and sell when you're 43. Then, when you're 60, you sell that home and move to a third home. That's three homes in 32 years.

Now, let's look at some possible numbers. To simplify the discussion, we're assuming that all purchase and sale prices here are adjusted. We're going to say the first home was bought for $28,175 and sold for $79,250; the profit was $51,075. The second home was bought for $94,450 and sold for $108,190. And the third home was bought for $121,200. Note that each purchase price in this example is higher than the sale price of the previous property. This is a requirement for deferral of all the taxes. Here's how the numbers break down:

Purchase price, first home	$28,175
Sale price, first home	79,250
Profit on sale	$51,075

Purchase price, second home	$ 94,450
Less: deferred profit, first home	51,075
Adjusted basis, second home	$ 43,375
Sale price, second home	$108,190
Profit on sale	$ 64,815
Purchase price, third home	$121,200
Less: deferred profit, second home	64,815
Adjusted basis, third home	$ 56,385

To this point, no taxes are due on these transactions, even though the owner has traded up and made a profit each time. The deferred profit simply reduces the basis of each subsequent purchase. And remember the once-in-a-lifetime exclusion rule. For example, let's say the owner sells this property for $176,700, and does not reinvest the profits anywhere. As long as the owner is over 55 and meets the other requirements of the rule, there will still be no taxes due on the profit:

Adjusted sale price	$176,700
Less: adjusted basis in the home	56,385
Profit	$120,315

Since this profit is less than $125,000, exercising the exclusion means no taxes will be due.

Whenever you sell your home, you are required to file an information schedule with your federal income tax return. (Consult with your tax adviser for state income tax requirements.) Form 2119, "Sale or Exchange of Principal Residence," includes four separate sections. They deal with:

1. Qualification for deferral and exclusion of tax

2. Computation of gain

3. Gain to be postponed (deferred) and calculation of the adjusted basis on your new home

4. 55-or-older exclusion

This form must be filed with your tax return for the year in which your residence is sold, whether or not you have replaced it with another home at the time you file. You have two years to qualify for the deferral of taxes on profits. If you are planning to buy or build a new home within that deadline, you complete only the first two sections of the tax form. The gain is not included in your taxable income. When you do buy or build your new home, you send in an amended Form 2119.

If you do not plan to replace your residence, you compute the gain on Form 2119 and include it in your taxable income, paying taxes for the current year.

If you originally planned not to replace your home and you paid a tax, and then changed your mind, you will need to file an amended tax return. You would file federal Form 1040X and apply for a refund. If you lose money on the sale, you do not have to file any returns. However, it is advisable to fill out Form 2119 just to document the fact that you have no gain to report. To find out more about the tax rules concerning the sale of your home, contact your local IRS office and ask for a free copy of Publication 523, "Selling Your Home."

22

Vacation Homes

At some time, many homeowners consider buying a second home—for the enjoyment of owning a getaway place in the mountains, on the lake, or in the woods. According to the U.S. Census Bureau, approximately 4 million people in the United States buy a second home. That represents less than 4 percent of all homeowners.

Before buying a vacation home, ask yourself these questions:

- Are you sure you want to spend most of your vacations in one spot? You might discover that you want to go to other places at times, but due to the cost of the second home, you might feel obligated to always vacation there.
- Do you really want to deal with year-round taxes and upkeep, not to mention mortgage payments, on a place you'll use only seasonally? Be sure to compare the real costs of buying a second home to the benefits. If it's just a matter of saving a hotel bill for one or two weeks a year, go over the numbers again.
- Can you afford the down payment? For second homes, lenders may require larger down payments than for principal residences. You should also know that the mortgage rate might be higher as well.

- How long or how difficult is the trip to the location of the vacation home—especially during peak vacation hours? If the home is located at a popular vacation site, you might find yourself in a massive commute every time you take your vacation.
- Do you have the temperament to cope with the financial responsibility of two mortgages and two property tax bills? Even if you use the second home only occasionally, the bills will come due with regularity.
- Are you willing to put up with relatives and friends who want to share your vacation or use your second home whenever you're not there? Like a swimming pool, a second home attracts new friends you didn't even know you had.

In other words, is the whole idea worth it? For some, it is; for others, a study of the numbers might reveal that there will likely be more headaches than benefits. You might feel so refreshed by the change in scenery, and you might love the area so much, that the expense, responsibility, and inconveniences are worth it. You might also justify the extra burden by thinking of the second home as a retirement homesite or investment. Even so, take a hardheaded attitude in analyzing your possible Shangri-la; only with careful planning and a realistic outlook will buying your second home be a successful personal and financial decision.

■ Renting out Your Vacation Home

You might justify your investment in a second home by renting it out for part of the year. This could be a problem if, in fact, the demand for such a house is only seasonal. Consider: Why do you go to that area? Is it popular only during the warmest part of summer? Or is there rental demand year-round?

The tax laws complicate your ability to get maximum tax advantage from a second home. First, the benefits: You are allowed to deduct all of the interest you pay on the mortgage for a second home, subject only to the restrictions explained previously. Property taxes are also deductible on Schedule A, Itemized Deductions, as part of your personal federal tax return. (Check the rules of your state for state deductibility.)

Vacation or second homes are subject to special federal rules. If you use the property for your own use for more than 14 days, it is considered a second residence. This rule involves an alternative computation. If you rent the home out for part of the year, and you use the home for personal use one-tenth of that time, it's considered a personal residence. For example, if you rent out the place for 120 days, and you use it for personal use 12 days or more (10 percent), then it's a personal residence. You use the greater of these two numbers to determine the status of the property.

Here's how it works: Let's say you used the house yourself for 16 days last year. Is it a personal residence? Under the first test, you have exceeded the minimum of 14 days. However, let's also assume that you rented out the property for 170 days. Ten percent would be 17 days; therefore, you *don't* meet that test. Since you are required to use the greater of the two numbers, in this case the second home would *not* be treated as a second home for residential purposes.

Another rule: If you rent out the place for fewer than 15 days during the year, you cannot treat it as a rental property. That means you can't deduct insurance, maintenance, and other costs. However, you can still deduct all your mortgage interest and property taxes as itemized deductions.

If you use the property as a personal residence (that is, for more than the greater of 14 days per year or a number of days equal to or greater than 10 percent of the total rental days), *and* you also rent the place out for more than 15 days during the year, you must report income and expenses on Schedule E of your tax return. However, you are not allowed to deduct all of your rental expenses, only that portion applied to the rental period. You have to separate personal expenses from rental expenses. Some expenses can be attributed directly to rental expenses, such as advertising to find a tenant. Other expenses can be broken down by formula.

The best formula to use involves a percentage allocation of rental time. Let's say you rent out property for 105 days per year. The fraction of the year during which expenses are related to rentals is 105/365.

You are allowed to deduct the exact portion of taxes and interest that apply to rental income, even if those exceed the amount of income. However, you are only allowed to deduct other expenses, including depreciation, to the extent that those expenses don't exceed the difference between rental income and rental expenses already deducted. In other words, if you use your vacation home as a personal residence as well as for rental, you might not be able to deduct net losses.

The nonrental portion of interest and taxes are deductible as itemized deductions, while the part attributable to rental time is to be included on Schedule E. Publication 527, available free from the IRS, includes a complete discussion of these calculations. If you are thinking of buying a second home and renting it out part of the year, it's worth reading up on these rather complex rules.

If you do *not* use the second home as a personal residence (that is to say, for the greater of 14 days per year or a number of days equal to or greater than 10 percent of the days it is rented out), and you rent out the property, you may be able to deduct all of your rental expenses, even if they exceed your rental income. You should speak to your tax adviser to ensure that you report all rental income and expenses from a second home in compliance with current federal (and state) rules.

Let's review these rules with some examples:

Example 1: On January 1, 1996, you bought a vacation condominium for $150,000, paying $30,000 in cash and financing $120,000. You used the condominium for your personal use for 10 days, and rented it out for 90 days. Your income and expenses for the year were:

	Total	Rental (90%)	Personal (10%)
Rental income	$ 5,000	$ 5,000	$ 0
Taxes	(2,000)	(1,800)	(200)
Mortgage interest	(12,000)	(10,800)	(1,200)
Common area charges	(2,000)	(1,800)	(200)
Depreciation	(5,000)	(4,500)	(500)
Net	$(16,000)	$(13,900)	$(2,100)

Your adjusted gross income for the year, not including the use of the property, was $165,000. There is no other passive income or loss.

In this case, you had a potential loss of $13,900 from renting the condominium. Since you did not personally use the property for more than the greater of 14 days or 10 percent of the number of rental days, your loss is not limited by the vacation home rules. However, your deduction *is* restricted by the passive loss activity rule.

Example 2: Same facts as in Example 1, except that you used the condominium for personal use for 20 days, and rented in out for 80 days. You designate the condominium as your secondary residence for the purpose of deducting mortgage interest. Your income and expenses break down as:

	Total	Rental (80%)	Personal (20%)
Rental income	$ 5,000	$ 5,000	$ 0
Taxes	(2,000)	(1,600)	(400)
Mortgage interest	(12,000)	(9,600)	(2,400)
Subtotal	(9,000)	(6,200)	(2,800)
Common area charges	(2,000)	(1,600)	(400)
Depreciation	(5,000)	(4,000)	(1,000)
Net	$(16,000)	$(11,800)	$(4,200)

In this case, you can deduct $1,600 in taxes and $9,600 in mortgage interest on Schedule E. Because you used the condominium for more than 14 days in the year, and taxes and interest are higher than rental income, you may not deduct any of the remaining rental expenses. You can deduct on Schedule A the remainder of both your property tax expense ($400) and your interest expense ($2,400).

Example 3: Same facts as in Example 1, except that you have an adjusted gross income of $75,000 before considering the losses from rental activity and no other profit or loss from real estate or other passive activities. You actively participate in the management of the condominium.

In this example, you can deduct on Schedule E your entire loss of $13,900 from renting out the condominium, in addition to your deductions of taxes and interest on Schedule A.

■ Time-Sharing

Time-sharing is one way to own part of a vacation home. You have the right to use the property for a specified period of time each year, usually identified by precise dates. However, before you buy a time-share, you should be aware of a few facts.

The average week costs $7,800 to buy, with an annual maintenance fee of $316. In addition, owners have discovered that there is virtually no market for purchasing their used time-shares. (You may have the right to swap your specified week with someone else, assuming anyone else is willing to swap.) A 1992 survey conducted by Resort Property Owners Association revealed that 58 percent of time-share owners wanted to sell, but only 3 percent were able to.

Most time-shares fall in value, so even if you can find another buyer to take your time-share, you may lose money. And when you consider how little use you will get, it's an expensive way to take a vacation.

Anyone who has vacationed in Mexico has undoubtedly seen ads or been approached with promises of affordable, luxury homes high on a hill overlooking the beach, for virtually no money. Most of these are overpriced and have no resale market. Before buying a time-share, consider that you may be stuck with it forever. If you use it every year, are certain you can go on vacation on exactly the same dates each time, and are willing to go to the same place, a time-share *might* be right for you. But also be realistic. Using the average cost of $7,800 plus $316 per year in maintenance, if you use your time-share every year for ten years, the cost of your weekly vacation is:

$7,800 / 10	=	$ 780
Maintenance	=	316
Weekly cost	=	$1,096

Now, ask yourself: Can you find a decent accommodation in the same place for *less* than $1,096 each year? Chances are there are plenty of available bargains, probably with the round-trip airfare thrown in, too. And you will have the freedom of going on vacation whenever you like, not just during your one week of time-share rights each year.

Other Ways to Own a Home

23

Mobile Homes

Today, one out of every 16 Americans lives in a mobile home. Of all forms of housing, this is the fastest-growing category. The figure doesn't include campers, vans, and trailers, which are classified as recreational vehicles and not as homes.

Mobile homes are for many a viable choice for a first home, simply because they are much more affordable than permanent housing. Remember, though, that part of the investment benefit of home ownership comes from appreciating land values. More than half of all mobile-home owners do not own the land on which they live.

Based on the latest prices, mobile homes cost about one-third less than typical homes—mainly because of the lower land costs and the generally smaller size of mobile homes. According to the U.S. Bureau of the Census, about 245,000 new mobile homes are constructed each year, at an average cost of $31,000. In 1950, mobile homes accounted for seven-tenths of 1 percent of total housing. The rise by decade has been steady. In 1960, 1.4 percent; in 1970, 2.9 percent; in 1980, 4.8 percent; and the latest statistics, for 1993, show that about 7 percent of the housing market is made up of mobile homes.

These statistics are summarized in Figure 23.1 on page 215.

■ Demographic Breakdowns

No one age group dominates the mobile-housing market, although it is most popular among the very young who cannot afford other forms of housing. Some senior citizens do opt to sell their homes and move to mobile-home parks marketed for people in the retirement ages, but such movement has not shown up dramatically in the statistics.

The median age of a mobile-home owner is 44. However, the broad breakdown of mobile-home ownership shows that the largest age concentration is between ages 25 and 44:

Under 25	6.2%
Ages 25 to 44	44.9
Ages 45–64	26.2
Age 65 and up	<u>22.7</u>
Total	100.0

This breakdown shows that the trend is *not* the same as it is in single-family housing, condominium, and co-op markets. In other words, mobile homes are not thought of as retirement housing, nor is there a growing tendency to become a mobile-home owner with age. Although housing ownership rates rise with age, ownership rates for mobile homes tend to have less representation by retirement age, rather than more.

■ Tax Considerations

The 1980 Federal Housing Act identified mobile homes by the title "manufactured housing." In today's housing market, many permanent homes placed on foundations are "manufactured" but are not mobile homes.

Technically, a mobile home is not real estate but rather a form of personal property. That means that lenders view mobiles differently than they view land and buildings. Financing may be available at higher rates (see the discussion later in this chapter) and with a higher required down payment. That's because mobile-home values depreciate over time, whereas permanent housing values increase. There is a trend among some lenders to treat high-quality mobile homes the same as permanent housing, especially if the owners also finance or already own the land. As we already mentioned, that qualification covers only about one-half of all mobile-home owners.

Even though mobile homes are not viewed by lenders as favorably as permanent housing, the IRS makes no distinction. For purposes of the tax deferral rules and for the once-in-a-lifetime over-55 exclusion of gain, mobile homes are treated like any other primary residence—as long as

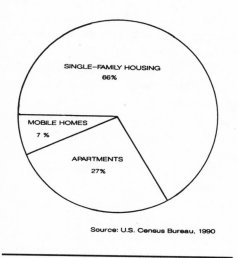

Source: U.S. Census Bureau, 1990

Figure 23.1 Housing Ownership by Type

they contain cooking, sleeping, and sanitary facilities. You are also allowed to deduct loan interest as mortgage interest, as well as property taxes—at least on your federal tax return. Rules for deductibility for state income tax returns vary by state.

■ Financing and Market Value

The attraction of the mobile home is its low cost compared with other housing. But mobile homes are financed more like automobiles than like houses. And there is a good reason why. Like a car, a mobile home loses between 20 and 50 percent of its value during the first five years. Some lenders offer competitive rates for mobile-home mortgages, but as a general rule, conventional loans average five percentage points higher for mobile-home mortgages than for traditional home mortgages. Therefore, if a single-family home mortgage is marketed at 8 percent, a mobile home's rate might be as high as 13 percent.

Whereas standard housing appreciates in value, mobile-home values fall. For this reason, lenders will not only expect more money down—20 percent or more—and a higher interest rate, they often will finance a mobile home over a shorter term, usually only 10 years.

Although you will pay less interest in a shorter-term mortgage, the higher rate and higher monthly payments may be a strain on a family's budget, especially considering the tendency for mobile-home owners to be younger than the average single-family homeowner.

However, this doesn't mean there's no hope of getting a competitive loan. The Federal Housing Administration (FHA) and the Veterans Administration (VA) offer low-interest, 15-year loans for mobile homes meeting minimum standards for size, price, and quality of construction. Shop around with other lenders. Some are willing to compete with rates and terms to get your business.

The ability to get a competitive loan depends on the quality and price of the unit, as well as where it's placed. Owning the land beneath the mobile home increases your chances for a low-rate loan. If the mobile unit is in an unpaved, overcrowded mobile-home park in a high-crime area, or in between a freeway and a quarry, the value will be low and prospects for a competitive loan will be dim. However, if you locate your brand new, well-built mobile home in a peaceful, security patrolled mobile-home park with plenty of space between units, paved streets, and landscaped common areas and buffers, you have a vastly better chance for getting the loan you want.

■ Advantages and Disadvantages

Mobile homes offer several advantages over single-family housing and condos or co-ops. These include:

- They cost less, primarily because land is not included in the price, and the typical size is much smaller than the size of a single-family home. The average size of a mobile home is 906 square feet, compared with 1,688 square feet for other housing. (The mobile-home owner usually has two bedrooms, a living area, and either one or two bathrooms.)
- They are good starter homes. On average, owners of mobile homes earn $18,758 per year, which is considerably less than the average American family's income of $27,735.
- Mobiles are good alternatives for empty nesters—couples whose children have grown and left home. Mobiles are easier and cheaper to maintain. If you need less space than you presently have in your home, a mobile home might make a lot of sense.

And if you're over 55, you can take advantage of the over-55 rule to sell a home without being taxed.

- The environment of a well-maintained mobile-home park is well suited for social contact, allowing you to make new friends readily.
- Monthly common fees include water and garbage service in most cases, maintenance of common areas, and, possibly, access to a clubhouse and swimming pool.
- High-quality mobile-home construction is becoming the norm, and newly purchased units come with at least a one-year warranty (required by federal law).

You will also have certain disadvantages:

- Mobile homes generally have poor investment value. Lower-priced units and those in lower quality parks will decline in value by as much as half the purchase price within the first few years. The only investment benefit mobile-home owners have is when they also own the land. (The majority do not own the land but pay rent for their space.)
- Mobile-home sellers might have problems finding suitable buyers, since many would-be homeowners shy away from this market. New units are so affordable that there is only a limited market for used mobiles and, if the park is not of the highest quality, most people will not be impressed.
- Lot and common area fees may be raised. They range between $30 and $500 per month, possibly more in the highest-quality parks. The better the environment, the higher the cost. And if residents elect to hire a security company, put in electronic gates, or install other expensive measures, fees may rise even more.
- Mobile homes are not always well constructed. Even with a one-year warranty—some offer up to five years—some manufacturers have been notoriously slow in responding to complaints. The most common problems are poor insulation and leaking roofs.
- Mobile homes are exceptionally vulnerable to fire and windstorm damage.
- Financing alternatives are limited.
- Many mobile-home parks are in areas zoned commercial-industrial. This might mean the park is situated too near industrial sites.

■ Buying Recommendations

The following guidelines should be kept in mind when shopping for a mobile home:

Check the appearance of the park. The quality of life in a mobile-home park will be extremely important in the long run, so you should be aware of the surroundings. Make sure that streets are paved, ample space is provided between units, and all common areas are well maintained.

Examine the location. Is the park in a quiet area, well away from freeways, railroad tracks, and busy streets? Also, look for a park conveniently close to shopping, transportation, churches, and other points of interest.

Compare park rules and fees. Find out how often fees have been increased. Be sure the park rules won't restrict your ability to sell the mobile home later, and that you won't be required to buy a specified model from only one dealer. Are there any entrance fees? If so, how much? Are you charged extra fees for hooking up utilities? How long is the land lease? Do you have the option to buy the land? What are the park rules regarding visitors and pets?

Look into local financing. Before committing yourself to buying a mobile home or the land it sits on, visit several lenders and determine what financing terms are available. Shop around, and don't overlook FHA and VA loans.

Reserve a lot space before you buy. Never purchase a mobile home until you have reserved (or purchased) a lot space in a mobile-home park that you have thoroughly checked out.

Buy quality construction. Wood construction is preferred over other materials. The better the quality, the more comfortable you will be in your mobile home, and the longer the home will retain its value.

Examine your warranty. Manufacturers are required to provide you with a one-year warranty, and some provide warranties for a longer term. Be sure you know in advance of purchase exactly what limitations and exclusions apply, and determine the procedure for filing a warranty claim.

Ask about extra costs. Will the manufacturer charge you for transporting the mobile home to your new site, for setting it up, or for providing extra insurance? What other costs are involved? Who pays for hooking up electricity and plumbing? If you're financing the purchase, what are the closing costs? Will you be required to pay sales tax or registration, and how much?

Consider a used model. Because mobile homes tend to decline in value, you might find a bargain on the used market. Chances are, there are more used units for sale than there are interested buyers, meaning you have an advantage. Be sure the unit was well-maintained and that it isn't being sold because of problems. Be sure the unit was manufactured after 1976, when the Department of Housing and Urban Development began requiring minimum safety and quality standards for mobile-home construction.

Install safety extras. Securely anchor your home, whether it is required by state law or not. Install smoke detectors, and keep a fresh battery in them. In addition, have two or more fire extinguishers on hand, with one in the kitchen area.

Buy the right insurance. Shop around for good rates, but don't hesitate to pay extra for insurance coverage if a standard mobile-home policy doesn't adequately cover your possessions or provide protection against windstorm. Buy extra liability coverage if you believe the standard policy level isn't high enough.

24

Condominiums
and Cooperatives

■ Condominiums

It might be difficult to believe, but in the early 1960s, "condominiums," or "condos," were hardly household words. There were few condo developments, and those in existence were primarily in retirement or resort communities. A 1975 survey conducted by the Department of Housing and Urban Development revealed that, at that time, there were 14,000 condominium developments in the United States. Half of those were located in only three states: Florida, California, and New York. By 1985, according to an updated version of the same study, more than 60,000 condominium projects totaled more than 3 million units. According to the Chicago Title Insurance Company, in 1992, 13 percent of all households were condominiums. The National Association of Realtors reports that 65 percent of all condominium owners are first-time buyers. In areas where condos are attractive, they are primarily considered starter-home markets.

Prices of condos vary by region. In many areas, condo prices are on a par with single-family housing. In large cities, condos and co-ops are considered luxury housing, while well-constructed condominium units—often in large-scale developments with pools and tennis courts—

are popular in suburbs and among younger single-home buyers. They also appeal to the large segment of divorced people who want to own property while reducing maintenance and upkeep. Because condominiums can usually be leased out, many homeowners find condos to be convenient second or vacation homes.

The condominium idea has appeal because of the combination of ownership features and shared expense features. What do you actually buy when you buy a condominium? The Department of Housing and Urban Development calls condominiums "air-space estates." As a condo owner, you don't own the building or the land, only the air space within the walls of one unit. You own all the finished surfaces on the walls, such as wallpaper or paint, but not the walls themselves; you own the light fixtures and carpeting, but not the ceilings or floors. Everything *within* the confines of the unit is yours—you receive a deed for it and the exact amount of space you purchase is recorded in your name.

The rest of the development—hallways, grounds, club room, swimming pool, lobby, building, and land—is called "undivided interests," and all owners share these elements communally.

A condominium is a self-governing community run by an elected condo board of directors. Whereas each unit is owned individually, the common interests of all the owners are protected and managed by the group through its board.

A condominium association is created to elect a board of managers or directors. Each unit owner is a member of the association and can vote for board members. The number of votes you own depends on the percentage of interest you have in the total property.

Some associations base voting rights strictly on square feet within a unit. Voting shares can also be allocated based on square feet modified by the relative desirability of each unit's location—floor level, views, or buffers from traffic.

The board's duties and rights include:

- Establishing an operating budget
- Collecting maintenance fees for common areas
- Enforcing fee collection
- Placing liens on the property of delinquent owners
- Distributing billings and notices
- Keeping members informed

- Creating and enforcing rules for members
- Conducting periodic meetings
- Acting on improvement requests from owners
- Paying liability and casualty insurance premiums
- Approving needed common area maintenance bills
- Complying with state and local laws

The board usually has the right to approve or turn down an improvement proposed by an owner. The bylaws probably explicitly forbid you from making any improvements without first getting permission, even within your own unit. Be sure to check how restrictive the bylaws are *before* you buy a condo. In some developments, you might not be able to get anything approved, even if it's only a small deck outside your back door or a kitchen counter.

The board cannot restrict you from selling your unit to anyone you want and cannot dictate lease terms if you decide to turn your unit into a rental. Some associations hold a "right of first refusal," meaning that if you decide to sell, they have the first chance at making an offer. Check the bylaws thoroughly before buying, and consider having your attorney review the documents for you.

The board also enforces the rules of conduct within the development, meaning they restrict business uses, noise after certain hours, and the usage of common areas.

■ Cooperative Housing

Cooperative apartments, or co-ops, are not an especially popular housing alternative in the United States, except in the larger urban centers in the east and northeast. In 1994, there were 96,000 purchases of co-up units. For most Americans, condominiums are far more desirable than co-ops.

While there are many similarities between the two types of housing, there are also some important distinctions. When you own a cooperative apartment unit, you are not the owner of any real property, but of shares in the corporation which, in turn, owns the entire complex. The buyer acquires the shares allocated to the unit (these vary depending on size and location within the development) and acquires a proprietary lease. Unlike the condo board, a co-op corporation typically holds a mortgage on the entire property. Monthly charges include not only shared maintenance and insurance costs, but principal and interest payments as well.

Voting rights in the co-op are determined in the same way as those in the condominium—based on the number of shares each owner has. However, if you are financing your share purchase, your rights as an investor *and* your risks may be affected. Some co-op boards limit the amount of outside financing they allow for share purchases, and may also restrict your voting rights. To buy a co-op, you may be required to come up with a fairly large amount of cash.

Compared with condos, co-op boards have more control over share purchasers. The co-op board has the right to approve or disapprove a prospective buyer, and can also forbid you to sublet your unit. Some boards will be more flexible than others, and as the market weakens, the tendency is to relax the rules. As with condos, the rules of the co-op should be thoroughly investigated before you attempt to buy in.

Besides paying off part of the mortgage, co-op shareholders are required to pay a portion of monthly maintenance, security, insurance, and building management expense. Your share of interest for the underlying mortgage loan is deductible on your itemized tax return if the unit is your primary or secondary residence.

Co-op shareholders face the risk of rising maintenance expenses, meaning monthly housing rates can rise over time. This is not a problem unique to co-ops. All homeowners face the risk of rising utility, insurance, and maintenance expenses, although single-family owners have more control. (Single-family owners can defer maintenance if they choose; the condo and co-op owner cannot because such decisions are made in behalf of all owners by the board.) You should ask your attorney to review the bylaws, the proprietary lease, and the most recent financial statement of the co-op, and ask for a building inspection of the unit before agreeing to buy.

As a co-op investor, you have exclusive rights to the use of your apartment as well as common areas, just as with a condo. Like condo boards, co-op boards restrict alterations or improvements to individual units. You need permission in advance of any major renovations.

The benefits of co-op living include tax advantages like writing off your share of interest and property taxes; the economy of shared maintenance expenses and insurance; and the enjoyment of an urban lifestyle without expensive upkeep.

▪ Buying a Condo or Co-op

You can buy a condo or co-op in one of three ways. First, you can buy a unit from a member of an existing association or development; second, you can be among the first buyers in a new development; and third, you can purchase a conversion unit as an "insider" tenant. Each of these three methods has its own distinct advantages and disadvantages.

Unit in an existing development. Established condo or co-op developments offer you the advantage of having already gone through the start-up period. The board should be an operating group that knows what it's doing. Any initial construction problems should have been solved long ago; even so, you should plan to hire your own independent building inspector and get a written report before buying. Be sure the inspector looks not only at the building and the unit but also at mechanical systems such as heating and air-conditioning.

Also, speak to the building maintenance superintendent or manager to determine the maintenance history of the building itself. Has the board voted for any maintenance budget increases? Have repairs and maintenance been performed regularly? Or is the board deferring work, allowing the building and systems to degenerate?

In addition, ask to see the latest financial statement of the association. Review the bylaws with your attorney, and ask questions about the frequency of common area fee increases. Also, make sure you know all the rules by which you will be expected to live. Be sure you're not just buying someone else's problems.

First buyer in a new development. Buying a unit in a new development gives you the advantage of being able to benefit from any immediate appreciation in value once the development becomes fully occupied. That happens as long as there is a healthy market demand. (If demand slackens, unit values will stabilize or could drop.) As one of the first owners, you and others in the same situation will have to contend with the initial problems that arise, including structural problems and uncompleted work by the contractor.

Developers or sponsors initially control the board of directors until there are enough other owners to constitute a majority. Make sure that your prospectus, association bylaws, or proprietary lease calls for the developer to give up control once 51 percent or more of the units have been sold. Otherwise, the developer may exercise control over the entire complex for an unreasonably long time. Also, before you buy, try to determine the level of monthly maintenance charges. In some cases, developers have set unrealistically low fees to attract buyers (a practice called lowballing). Later, when the developer has gone, you and your fellow owners may realize that you need to pay a lot more to cover the insurance and maintenance costs. Check the monthly fees of other associations in the same area with the same approximate number of units, to judge whether the fees in the development are realistic.

Purchasing a conversion unit. Many condo and co-op units were once rental apartments. If your rental apartment building is undergoing a conversion to condo or co-op status, you might be able to purchase your unit at a below-market price as an inside tenant. The conversion process can be frustrating and complicated. Here are the main points to think about:

- Condition of the building or buildings. Are you buying a lot of deferred maintenance with the purchase of your unit? Will future repair and maintenance costs drastically increase your financial burden? More than with any other type of purchase, you need a building inspection before deciding to buy a conversion unit.
- Price of the unit. How does the asked price compare with similar condo or co-op units on the market?
- Location of the building or complex: Does the location ensure high probability of continued market demand? Location has much to do with future market value.
- Current market conditions. Is this a good time to buy? Is there a high demand for condo and co-op units or are many such units sitting on the market? In a slow market, you might have considerably more bargaining room as a buyer.
- Your income level. Can you afford to buy? Can you qualify for financing? Will your immediate and future income level provide you with the ability to support mortgage payments that might exceed current levels of rent, plus monthly maintenance fees?

If you receive a preliminary prospectus for a conversion plan, contact the state attorney's office and request information concerning your tenant rights during conversions. Also, check your city or county housing board for similar information.

Get the tenants in the building or complex organized into a group association that can respond effectively to the sponsor's plan. The key to a successful conversion for tenants is organizing a tenants' association. You can collectively hire a building inspector to help you decide whether or not to convert. The tenants can then ask the owner to make needed repairs before agreeing to a conversion contract. You and your fellow tenants should also retain an attorney to review current law as well as the offer the owner makes.

■ Other Facts on Condo or Co-op Ownership

Maintenance. Unlike rental living, as the owner of a condo or co-op unit, you are responsible for the daily maintenance and upkeep of your unit. If a leak develops in a faucet in your unit, you must get it repaired. However, if the leak comes from a unit above yours, the association is normally responsible for paying for it—as a shared common area expense. The association also assumes responsibility for repairing the roof, painting the outside of the building, and keeping hallways and lobbies in good condition.

Insurance. Insurance coverage in a condo or co-op development is fairly evenly divided between unit owners and the association. Generally, the interior of your unit is your responsibility and, as a homeowner, you should carry enough insurance to cover your personal property and liability. The association is responsible for the building and grounds insurance, including liability coverage for all owners as a whole.

The management company. The board of directors of a condo or co-op may hire a professional real estate company to oversee the functioning of the building, the hiring of maintenance employees or contractors, and the handling of special problems that arise from time to time. This is most likely to happen in larger complexes, where management is a full-time job. The management company is responsible for keeping the books and preparing budget and financial reports for the board, as well as for collecting monthly fees from each unit owner.

Taxes. If the condo or co-op is your primary or secondary residence, you are allowed to deduct the mortgage interest you pay directly (for co-ops, you can deduct your share of the corporation's payments). You can also deduct property taxes on your itemized tax return.

Glossary
of Real Estate Terms

Abstract of title: a summary of the ownership history of a property, including changes in ownership, current mortgages outstanding, liens, charges, and other holds on the title.

Acceleration clause: a stipulation in a loan agreement stating that the entire balance will be payable immediately to the lender upon failure of the owner to make timely payments or meet other requirements.

Adjustable-rate mortgage (ARM): a mortgage loan agreement which provides that the interest rate will be changed periodically, based on changes in the rate in a specified index.

Adjusted sales price: the sales price of a property, minus commissions and other closing costs, and minus any fix-up expenses.

After-tax cost: the true cost of owning property after calculating the reduction of tax liabilities resulting from deducting interest and property taxes.

Agent: an individual who has been given the power to act on behalf of another. A real estate agent is licensed by the state to work in affiliation with a broker.

All-risk form: the most popular form of homeowner's insurance, including coverage for all perils except specific, named exclusions. Also known as HO-3.

Amortization: the reduction of a loan's balance by periodic payments. The portion of each payment assigned to principal amortizes (reduces) the mortgage balance.

Appraisal: the examination of property by a professional for the purpose of estimating the current market value, usually based on comparisons to recently sold homes similar in size, features, and neighborhood.

Appreciation: the growth in market value of property over time, as a result of increases in market demand and value.

Assessment: valuation of property for the purpose of taxation, or a special-purpose tax.

Assignment: delegation of rights and responsibilities to another, such as a lessee in his or her relationship with a sublessee.

Assumable mortgage: a mortgage loan allowing the seller of a property to transfer the loan to a buyer with the same terms, interest rate, and other conditions. Some assumable loans are subject to certain limitations.

Balloon mortgage: a form of financing calling for interest-only payments or payments with very low principal payments, with a large, single payment due at the end of a term, often three to five years.

Basic policy: a form of homeowner's insurance covering only certain named perils. Also called HO-1.

Basis: for tax purposes, a buyer's net cost of property, including adjustments for costs. Basis is used to compute taxable capital gain.

Binder: (1) a contract between buyer and seller of real estate specifying the primary features of their agreement, to be replaced later with a formal real estate contract; (2) a statement from an insurance company to a lender verifying that homeowner's insurance is in force on a property.

Blanket mortgage: financing on more than one property under a single agreement.

Broad form: homeowner's insurance covering 18 named perils, also called HO-2.

Broker: an individual licensed by a state to represent sellers in real estate transactions directly or through agents and salespeople.

Buy-down: financing in which a developer arranges for a buyer to obtain a mortgage loan at below-market rates while the developer subsidizes a portion of interest. In exchange, the price of the property is normally increased above comparable properties.

Buyer's market: a market condition in which there are more sellers than buyers, forcing asking prices down and giving buyers an advantage.

Cap: a ceiling on the interest rate or rate of increase in periodic interest rates a lender can charge in an adjustable-rate mortgage.

Capital asset: property such as real estate, business assets, or investments, subject to capital gains tax.

Capital gain or loss: a gain or loss from the sale of a capital asset.

Casualty insurance: that part of a homeowner's policy protecting against losses from natural or accidental causes.

Closing: the final phase in a real estate transaction, in which title is transferred from seller to buyer in exchange for payment of mortgages and other claims and financing is established.

Closing statement: a written summary of the transfer of title in real estate, including itemization of all closing costs.

Commission: payments to agents, brokers, or salespersons for transacting real estate.

Compound interest: the accelerating effect of savings when interest is left on deposit; or in mortgage loans, the computation of interest on a monthly basis.

Comprehensive: the most expensive form of homeowner's insurance, with all-risk coverage, also called HO-5.

Condominium policy: homeowner's insurance including all-risk coverage for property but no coverage on the building, designed especially for condominium and co-op owners, also called HO-6.

Consideration: usually a sum of money. To be binding, a contract must contain consideration. For example, in exchange for transferring title, consideration is the purchase price to be paid.

Contingency offer: a stipulation in a contract, such as the sale of a buyer's current home, or agreement by the seller to perform specified repairs. The contract is not binding until all contingencies are satisfied and removed.

Conveyance: the document, such as a deed, by which property is officially transferred from seller to buyer.

Declaration of homestead: a document filed with the county recorder to protect all or part of a homeowner's equity in property so that, in the event of a forced sale, the owner will be ensured of retaining some equity.

Deed: the document used to record the transfer of ownership of property from seller to buyer.

Deed of trust: used in some states in place of a mortgage, this is the assignment of title to a lender until the loan is repaid.

Default: failure to make mortgage payments, resulting in possible foreclosure on the property.

Default insurance: often called *mortgage insurance,* a form of coverage lenders may require of homeowners carrying less than 20-percent equity. Homeowners are required to pay premiums. The insurance is designed to compensate lenders in the event of default.

Deferred gain: a delay in tax liability allowed by tax law on income or profits, such as the profit from selling a primary residence, as long as another house is bought or built within two years.

Depreciation: (1) the gradual decrease in real market value of property or other assets, due to wear and tear, obsolescence, and design; (2) the tax benefit by which owners of capital assets are allowed to claim deductions for a portion of the assets' cost basis.

Earnest money: a deposit of cash accompanying an offer to buy property, as a sign of sincerity and good faith.

Easement: the legal right to use or to cross land owned by another person.

Equity: the portion of a property's current market value owned by the owner, with the balance representing debts due to a lender.

Equity conversion: term used to describe reverse annuity mortgages, in which a property owner accepts cash payments over time in exchange for all or part ownership in the property.

Equity line of credit: funds borrowed by homeowners to be used at their discretion. Only that portion used is subject to interest.

Escrow: the temporary holding by a third party of deposited funds, pending completion of title search and other steps in a real estate transaction, including the meeting of all contract terms.

Exclusion rule: a once-in-a-lifetime provision in the tax law, allowing a homeowner aged 55 or older to earn a profit up to $125,000 tax-free on a principal residence.

FHA mortgage: financing in which a loan granted by a conventional lender is insured by the Federal Housing Administration.

Fixed-rate mortgage: financing with a rate of interest fixed for the entire term.

Flexible-rate mortgage: alternative name for an adjustable-rate mortgage (ARM).

FmHA mortgage: financing in which a loan granted to a rural borrower is insured by the Farmers Home Administration.

Foreclosure: the legal process of taking property away from a buyer due to nonpayment of the mortgage.

Full amortization: the most common method of financing real estate, in which payments are calculated so that the loan will be fully paid by a specified date. Part of the payment goes to interest, part to principal, with the principal portion gradually increasing over time.

General contractor: a professional building or remodeling contractor responsible for completing a construction project directly, or for hiring subcontractors.

Graduated-payment mortgage: financing with payments increasing over a 5-year or 10-year period, with a variable rate of interest.

Growing-equity mortgage: a mortgage with a fixed interest rate and larger than normal payments. The excess is applied to principal.

Guaranteed loan: real estate financing including a guarantee against default, provided by the VA or FmHA.

Home-inspection service: a diagnostic service performed by a contractor or experienced individual or company to locate and explain defects in property.

Homeowner's insurance: coverage protecting homeowners from liability (damages to other people's property or from injuries suffered by others) and casualty (loss or damage due to fire, theft, natural disasters, and accidents).

Index: a measurement of interest rates, used to set increases or decreases in interest charged in an adjustable-rate mortgage.

Inflation: the increase in prices over time.

Insured loan: a loan granted by a conventional lender and insured against default by the FHA.

Interest: the cost of borrowing money.

Interest only: a provision in a mortgage providing that borrowers are required to make only interest payments each month.

Lease: an agreement between an owner and a tenant for a conveyance specifying a period of time and monthly liability, as well as other conditions.

Lease option: a method of buying real estate in which the buyer-to-be agrees to lease property for a period of time and at an established level. That buyer also pays for an option to purchase the property at a specified, set price by a specified date.

Legal description: identification of a property by exact location and boundaries.

Lessee: the tenant who occupies property under the terms of a lease.

Lessor: the owner of property, or landlord, who contracts with a lessee, or tenant, under the terms of a lease.

Leverage: the use of borrowed money to purchase property.

Liability insurance: protection against claims resulting from injury to others or damage to the property of others.

Lien: a claim against real estate in satisfaction of a debt, such as mortgage, back taxes, or work performed under contract.

Listing: a contract between a seller and a real estate broker giving the broker the right to act as listing agent on a piece of real estate.

Listing broker: a broker holding the original listing. Other brokers may sell the property through a Multiple Listing Service (MLS) arrangement; however, the listing broker is always entitled to part of the commission.

Loan origination fee: closing cost charged by a lender to process a mortgage loan application; often a substitute name for points charged to the borrower.

Long-term capital loss: loss from the sale of a capital asset that has been held for more than only a few months.

Low-rate mortgage: financing in which a large down payment is made, followed by a short period of payments with a below-market interest rate.

Market value: the current value of real estate that a buyer is willing to pay and that a seller is willing to accept.

Mortgage: a legal document specifying that the purchaser agrees to repay a loan according to the terms in a loan contract, placing a lien on the property until those conditions are met.

Mortgage acceleration: the process of paying off a loan more rapidly than required by contract; a higher amount is paid to principal each month, with the result that interest costs are reduced and the term for repayment is shortened.

Mortgage insurance: any of three types of insurance based on the balance due on a mortgage and levels of required monthly payments. (1) Mortgage life insurance: This pays off the mortgage balance in the event of the death of the homeowner. (2) Mortgage disability insurance: This form pays the monthly payment in the event of disability of the homeowner. (3) Mortgage default insurance: This pays all or part of the liability to the lender if the homeowner defaults and the lender is otherwise unable to recover the loan balance.

Multiple Listing Service (MLS): a real estate subscription service that publishes listings for the benefit of all member brokerage firms.

Notice to owner: a document given to homeowners by contractors advising them of state lien laws.

Offer: a proposal to purchase property specifying the price and other terms. If accepted, the offer's conditions form a real estate contract.

Plat book: a volume of maps and drawings of an area, showing location and boundaries of properties.

Point: an amount equal to 1 percent of the amount borrowed in a mortgage loan. Points are assessed by lenders as a form of additional interest, often a condition for granting a loan.

Prepayment penalty: a charge assessed against homeowners for early prepayment of a mortgage loan.

Principal: (1) the amount borrowed, or the portion of a loan remaining unpaid at any time; (2) the major party to a real estate transaction; (3) the individual responsible for overseeing the activities of agents, such as a real estate broker.

Promissory note: a written promise to repay a loan.

Property taxes: assessments paid by homeowners for schools, public works, and other costs of local and state government, based on the assessed valuation of property.

Proprietary lease: legal agreement between owner and a cooperative corporation that allows buyers to occupy their units.

Prorated expenses: those expenses paid at closing for amounts due to or from the individual buyers and sellers, divided according to the portion of a year or month each is responsible for. Typically, these include interest, property taxes, and utilities.

Prospectus: an offering plan issued by condominium and cooperative sponsors providing details of price, location, layout of units, financing, if available, and procedures and regulations of the development.

Rapid-payoff mortgage: financing with a fixed rate of interest and increased principal payments; this is also called a *growing-equity mortgage.*

Real estate broker: individual licensed by the state to represent homeowners in the selling of property, directly or through agents and salespeople.

Real estate sales agent: individual licensed by the state to represent the broker in a real estate transaction.

Real property: land, buildings, improvements, and permanent attachments.

Realtor: a real estate broker or agent who is a member of the National Association of Realtors.

Reconveyance: the return of property rights to homeowners upon satisfaction of a mortgage, lien, or other debt.

Recording: the official entry of transactions, liens, and reconveyances into the permanent record of a county.

Refinancing: paying off one mortgage loan by taking out another on the same property.

Renegotiable-rate mortgage: also called a *rollover,* mortgage with an agreed-upon rate of interest for a specified period of months or years. At the end of that period, lender and borrower must agree to new terms and interest rate, or the loan becomes due.

Renter's insurance policy: homeowner's insurance on possessions and improvements only, but excluding the building, also called HO-4.

Rent option: payment of a contractually agreed sum of money, part of which is for rent and part of which is to go toward a down payment to purchase the property at a later date.

Replacement value: provision in a homeowner's insurance policy guaranteeing that, without limitation, losses will be reimbursed at current replacement cost.

Reverse annuity mortgage (RAM): a form of equity conversion with two parts. First is the annuity, providing for monthly payments to the homeowner for a specified period or for life, based on the homeowner's age and value of the property. Second is the mortgage, which accumulates with interest based on annuity payments. At the end of the term, or upon death of the homeowner, the mortgage must be repaid or the house is converted to the company.

Rollover: a mortgage establishing interest rate and amount of monthly payment for a specified period of time, to be renegotiated later, also called a *renegotiable-rate mortgage.*

Second mortgage: a junior lien on property, a loan having only secondary claim behind the first mortgage in the event of default.

Seller's market: condition in which there are many people who want to buy but a limited supply of properties for sale. The effect is that prices rise due to the higher-than-normal demand.

Seller take-back: the provision by the seller of all or part of the financing upon sale of a property.

Shared-appreciation mortgage: unusual financing arrangement in which the lender allows below-market rates and payments in return for a share of profits upon the sale of the property.

Shared-equity mortgage: financing in which the down payment, monthly payments, and/or profits from the sale of the property are split between the owner and another party.

Subcontractor: person or company hired by a contractor or homeowner to complete certain portions of a home improvement.

Subdivision: a tract of land broken up into smaller plots for future homesites.

Sublease: arrangement entered into by a lessee of property with a tenant, in which the tenant makes payments to the lessee, who then makes payments to the lessor.

Survey: a measurement of the exact location and boundaries of property.

Tax bracket: also called the marginal tax rate, the percentage of taxable income a person pays.

Tax shelter: an investment allowing an individual to avoid or delay an income-tax liability.

Time-share: partially owned property, often for recreational use, in which the part-owner has the right to occupy property for a specified portion of the year, normally defined in one-week blocks.

Title: proof of ownership in real property.

Title insurance: protection insuring against the risk that undisclosed liens are placed on property. In that event, the title insurance policy will pay the lien. The premium is paid at closing, and the insurance remains in effect for as long as that owner has the property.

Title search: the process of examining the public record to discover all recorded liens, mortgages, and other claims against property.

Transfer fee: a closing cost for officially transferring ownership from seller to buyer.

Unconditional lien release: a document given to the homeowner by a contractor, freeing the homeowner from future liens from any suppliers or subcontractors.

VA mortgage: a mortgage granted by a conventional lender and guaranteed by the Veterans Administration; also called a GI loan.

Variable-rate mortgage: alternate name for an adjustable-rate mortgage (ARM).

Variance: an exception from the local zoning regulations.

Warranty: an assurance given by a home builder of the quality and condition of materials used in a home, good for a specified period of time; or coverage provided by a warranty company promising to pay for covered repairs.

Wraparound mortgage: form of financing in which the seller passes an assumable mortgage to the buyer and an additional second mortgage. The buyer pays the seller directly for both loans, and the seller then makes payments directly to the original lender.

Zoning: classifications of land use for different purposes, providing restrictions between residential, commercial, industrial, and recreational uses, and the means for enforcement of regulations by local government.

Index